THE
APPRENTICE
Witch's
SPELL BOOK

THE
APPRENTICE
Witch's
SPELL BOOK

SET YOUR INTENTIONS, UNLEASH YOUR POWER, AND CHANGE YOUR LIFE

MARIAN GREEN

Bluestreak
BOOKS

A QUARTO BOOK

This edition first printed in 2018 by

Bluestreak
BOOKS

Weldon Owen
Weldon Owen is a division of
Bonnier Publishing USA
1045 Sansome Street, Suite 100,
San Francisco, CA 94111
www.weldonowen.com

Library of Congress Cataloging in
Publication data is available.

ISBN: 978-1-68188-443-1

Conceived, edited,
and designed by
Quarto Publishing
an imprint of The Quarto Group
The Old Brewery
6 Blundell Street
London N7 9BH
www.quartoknows.com

QUA: 322542/304831

Editors: Steffanie Diamond Brown,
Tracie Lee Davis,
Claire Waite Brown
Designer: Michelle Pickering
Publisher: Samantha Warrington

Printed in China

CONTENTS

INTRODUCTION
8

The Magic of You 18

Going within the Mind Map 20

Walking the Hidden Paths 22

CHAPTER 1

ELEMENTAL MAGIC
24

Elementary Principles 26

The Spell of the Earth 30

The Magic of Water 32

The Being of Fire 34

Air for Inspiration 36

The Spirit of Sacred Space 38

CHAPTER 2

THE POWER OF
THE PLANETS
40

Calling on Planetary Help 42

The Sun: Inspiring
Inner Strength 46

The Moon of Mystery 48

Mercury: The Traveler 50

Venus: Lady of Love 52

Mars: The All-Powerful 54

Jupiter: Lord of Justice 56

Saturn: Lord of Time 58

Uranus: The Innovator 60

Neptune: Bringer of Sight 62

Pluto: Keeper of Memories 64

A Cosmos Spell 66

CHAPTER 3

THE MAGIC OF TIME
68

Time's Influence on Magic 70

Aries: The Ram 74

Taurus: The Bull 76

Gemini: The Twins 78

Cancer: The Crab 80

Leo: The Lion 82

Virgo: The Virgin 84

Libra: The Scales 86

Scorpio: The Scorpion 88

Sagittarius: The Archer 90

Capricorn: The Goat 92

Aquarius: The Water Carrier 94

Pisces: The Fish 96

CHAPTER 4

KITCHEN WITCHING
98

Magic from the Heart
of the Home 100

Make a Mint 104

Rosemary for Remembrance 106

Sage for Wisdom 108

Take Back Thyme 110

A Treasure Hunt 112

Harmony in the Kitchen 114

Lucky Spices 116

Pests Away 118

Chapter 5

DREAM WEAVING
120

Finding Insight in Dreams 122

Moon Sleep Spell 126

Nightmares Away 128

Sweet Dreams 130

Symbolic Dream Power 132

Dreaming the Day Away 134

Web of Dreams 136

A Letter from Your Soul 138

Dream Tea 140

Index 142

Credits 144

THE ARTS OF MAGIC AND WITCHCRAFT STEM FROM THE
VERY ROOTS OF HUMAN HISTORY, AND COMBINE SPELLS,
TALISMAN MAKING, AND THE USE OF AMULETS, TO WARD
OFF HARM OR TO BRING GOOD LUCK AND HEALTH.

INTRODUCTION

The earliest written records include prayers and spells calling for help from the gods, healing potions, observations of the stars, and descriptions of charms. This heritage would not have survived until today if it were useless. In modern times we understand the human mind better. We know that relaxation can assist creativity, and that our dreams can reveal solutions to problems. Today's witchcraft, therefore, combines this knowledge with the ancient traditions to attract magic forces and make our wishes come true.

THE TOOLS OF THE TRADE

It can be useful to look at the materials and techniques of ancient magic that are still used today. A spell is a collection of words, chanted, sung, or simply written, that asks for a specific kind of result. Spells are a simple form of magic, often used in conjunction with symbols and actions appropriate to the desired result or the god or power you are calling upon for help.

Talismans are made from precious jewels and valuable metals engraved with the words of spells. Incantations are chanted over them to empower them. Amulets are very ancient and used to protect a person or object. They are often shaped like an eye, to represent the eye of God that watches and protects. Charms are also physical objects, used to bring luck.

They are usually natural materials such as stones, plants, or herbs that have medicinal and magical qualities. An appropriate material can be wrapped in a particular colored silk to enhance its powers.

A pentagram (five-pointed star) made from twigs to represent the five elements: earth, water, fire, air, and spirit.

Amulets often feature a protective eye to watch over us.

USING SYMBOLS

The use of symbols with spells is the language by which we talk to the inner powers of our minds, to angels and gods who help us with our magic. Every tradition has symbols that need to be understood before they are used in spell weaving. Symbols, such as colors, scents, and metals, can relate to the desired effect of a spell, or to the power you are calling upon for assistance. One set of symbols that is widely used in modern charm making and spellcasting is that of the seven ancient planets. Below is a list of each planet's associations.

ANCIENT PLANET	DAY	METAL	COLOR	SCENT	
Sun	Sunday	Gold	Yellow	Frankincense	
Moon	Monday	Silver	White/Violet	Jasmine	
Mars	Tuesday	Iron	Red	Tobacco	
Mercury	Wednesday	Quicksilver	Orange	Copal	
Jupiter	Thursday	Tin	Blue	Cedar	
Venus	Friday	Copper	Green	Rose	
Saturn	Saturday	Lead	Black	Myrrh	

Rose water and a green candle in a copper holder are useful for spells invoking the help of Venus.

STONE	NUMBER	ZODIAC SIGN	ROMAN DEITY	GREEK DEITY
Diamond	6	Leo	Helios	Apollo
Moonstone	9	Cancer	Diana	Artemis
Bloodstone	5	Aries/Scorpio	Mars	Ares
Agate	8	Gemini/Virgo	Mercury	Hermes
Sapphire	4	Sagittarius/Pisces	Jupiter	Zeus
Emerald	7	Libra/Taurus	Venus	Aphrodite
Jet/Opal	3	Capricorn/Aquarius	Saturn	Chronos

Colored ribbons
are useful tools
for spell weaving,
such as green and
blue ribbons when
casting a spell for
career success.

SPELLCASTING

The spells described in this book are based on very ancient rules of colors, scents, numbers, materials, and symbols, so each spell specifies the tools used to empower the spoken spell, such as colored candles or ribbons, and incense. It is therefore imperative that you follow the instructions carefully. To learn the original rules takes many years, so to ensure the safety and effectiveness of the charms and magical acts here, old spells have been simplified and modernized for today's spell weavers. Before you cast a spell, the following points must be taken into consideration, to ensure safety and success:

✳ Each spell must be thoroughly thought out and used only for a single, specific objective at any one time. If it harms no one you may work your spell, but you do have to discover what your true need is, and then choose the best way of making it happen.

✳ Magic works for need not greed; it should bring you luck but will not bring you money.

✳ Spells only work if they are chanted with complete intent and focus. They are always very literal in their effect.

✳ These chants will only affect the person saying the spell, as to try to influence another person, even for what seems to be a good reason, is dark magic.

✳ Spell working uses the power of the trained and focused mind and can transform aspects of your life and the world around you, so make sure you are ready for change.

Your spells will not affect others against their will—you cannot make anyone fall in love with you.

✳ Spells may be worked by one person alone, or by a group of friends or a family, but everyone must be in agreement as to their purpose.

✳ Once the spell has been cast, the matter should be forgotten. It should be destroyed by fire and water once it has worked.

Wait for up to a lunar month for the effects of a spell to become manifest.

✳ Only work on one spell at a time, allowing between three days and a lunar month for some effect to be felt before going on to another.

✳ Much of this hidden knowledge is universal, so no matter where in the world you may be, it can be made to work.

BUILDING A BASE FOR MAGIC

Magic is a real force for change when applied properly. Just like electricity or gravity, it is difficult to explain or imagine, but anyone with a bit of patience and common sense can use it to alter the pattern of their lives. It is not necessary to believe in ancient gods and goddesses to make magic work, but you do need to keep an open mind, allowing yourself to accept that there are powers at work in the universe that can be helpful, without necessarily understanding how they work.

Most witches and magicians have their own ways of doing things. Their arts will have been built up through years of practice and the practical application of ancient methods to resolve the problems they face in their own lives, and those of the people who consult them. To make these techniques safe and effective for people who don't have years of training behind them, the spells in this book have been simplified. Those of you with more experience will see how you can alter, enlarge, and personalize these spells to make them fit your own level of expertise.

Practical magic can be traced back through witches, or wise women, to ancient times.

It is important that all newcomers to spell weaving practice the following basic skills to awaken their inner powers. These skills will greatly improve the effectiveness of your spellcasting.

CONCENTRATION

During spellcasting your focus should not be allowed to drift from the subject in hand. It is essential that you concentrate your mind pointedly on a particular subject, whether for a brief meditation or a long and complex spell. Complete concentration will help you send out a single, clear message to the powers that make spells work. A useful exercise to help you master the skill of concentration is to focus on the second hand of a watch, or the changing digits of an electronic clock, for one or two minutes. This is a useful technique that can be practiced while you are waiting for a train, for example, as most stations have a clock to concentrate on. It is, however, surprisingly difficult.

Focus on the second hand of a clock for two minutes to aid concentration.

Developing the ability to concentrate will help you to meditate and focus on your spellcasting.

Using a mirror
can help you to
visualize and
focus on the
desired result
of your spells.

Sit upright and
relaxed when
meditating and
visualizing.

MEDITATION

Meditation is a method of communicating
with the subconscious mind. It requires a
relaxed body with an alert mind, and will only
happen when you can deliberately shift levels
of consciousness. Meditation encourages
answers to questions, further information,
or realizations to spring into your awareness.
It is a passive state where these words and
ideas arise spontaneously, and it differs
from visualization.

    Sit upright and relax. Do not listen to
music. Close your eyes and concentrate on
your breathing, making it slow and deep.
Allow a feeling of calm and relaxation
to flow over you. Become still, letting all
distractions disappear. You are in control,
and will remain so. When you feel ready, put
the subject of the meditation—this may be a
problem you need to solve, a word, symbol, or
piece of text—into your inner awareness. The
idea must come ready formed to your mind.
Allow a train of thought to develop around
the basic concept, mentally noting the steps of
its progress. If your ideas go off the subject,
bring back your inner attention to the
words or symbol, and start again.

Gradually, you will find that your flying ideas slow down, and new concepts focused around the subject of your meditation begin to attract your attention.

Begin by practicing meditation for just ten minutes at a time, and allow this time to lengthen to a maximum of thirty minutes.

CREATIVE VISUALIZATION

An important part of magic is visualizing the result you desire. This is an active process, again performed in an altered state of consciousness, when the body is relaxed but the mind is alert. It is best to ground yourself by sitting still, with your spine straight and your head held upright on a relaxed neck and shoulders. Keep your head up so that you can breathe deeply and easily and not slump. Focus on an image and build up a clear picture of it, or for people who find it hard to see, focus on feelings about the subject. Create images in your imagination, describing such things as colors, shapes, atmosphere, landscapes, and so on. Practical exercises include reading books that vividly describe scenes or actions in a way that makes you feel you are a witness, or participating in them.

A note from the author

I was fortunate to grow up in the countryside where there were many people who still used the traditional herbal and magical arts on themselves and their animals. From them I learned about the powers of the planets and plants, the elements of earth, water, fire, and air, and many other things.

✳

To be able to use the magical arts, in the way it is written about in this book, is the result of over forty years of study, research, and practice where I have been instructed by witches, magicians, and wise country folk. These spells will work if you take them seriously and recognize that they are only a tiny part of a vast, ancient, and magical tradition.

A simple act of magic to illuminate your inner strengths.

✳

The MAGIC of YOU

OFTEN INSCRIBED OVER THE ENTRANCES TO VARIOUS TEMPLES IN ANCIENT GREECE, INCLUDING THE ORACLE AT DELPHI, WAS THE PHRASE "KNOW THYSELF." YOU CAN USE THIS SPELL AS A FIRST STEP TOWARD THIS PROCESS. BY EXAMINING YOUR OWN ACHIEVEMENTS AND FAILURES, WHICH ONLY YOU KNOW, YOU CAN CHANGE YOUR LIFE FOR THE BETTER. THIS PROCESS REQUIRES A LITTLE PATIENCE AND A LOT OF HONESTY, BUT IT IS WELL WORTH IT.

You will need

A green candle

✳

A recent photograph of yourself

✳

Paper and a pen

✳

A red envelope

METHOD

Light a green candle and, by its light, examine a recent photograph of yourself. Once you feel in touch with your image, take a piece of paper and fold it in half lengthwise. On the left-hand side of the paper, make a note of all the things you have always wanted to do, and whether you have done them at this point or not. On the right-hand side of the paper, write a list of things at which you have failed, and why.

─ ✳ ─

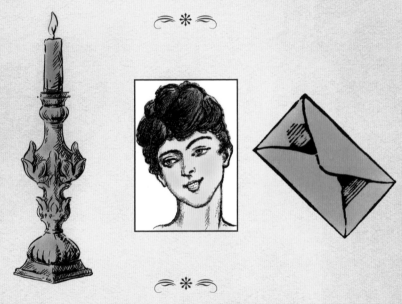

─ ✳ ─

When you feel the list is complete, tell your photograph how well you have done, despite your failures. Be positive. Select one unfulfilled ambition and promise yourself, solemnly, that you will take the first steps toward making it happen immediately. Pinch out the candle. Fold the list around the photograph, place them both in a red envelope, and hide the envelope in a drawer for one month. Repeat this process often.

Drawing a symbolic map of your life can result in a magical pattern that will reveal valuable insights.

≈ ❋ ≈

GOING within the MIND MAP

THE PLACES WE CALL HOME ARE USUALLY VERY DEAR TO OUR HEARTS, AND OFTEN REFLECT AN ESSENTIAL PART OF OUR VERY BEINGS. IN THIS SPELL, A MAP OF YOUR HOME AREA IS USED AS A TEMPLATE UPON WHICH TO DRAW A SYMBOLIC MAP OF YOUR LIFE. BY PLOTTING ALL THE LOCATIONS THAT PLAY AN IMPORTANT PART IN YOUR LIFE AND POSITIONING YOURSELF IN THE MIDDLE, YOU CAN DEVELOP A BETTER UNDERSTANDING OF YOUR PLACE IN THE WORLD. THIS INCREASED SELF-AWARENESS CAN IMPROVE YOUR CHANCES FOR SUCCESS IN LIFE.

METHOD

Spread a map of your home area out onto a flat surface. Spend exactly fifteen minutes drawing a pattern of your life onto the map, symbolically marking places like your school, your workplace, and the homes of your family and friends. Place yourself at the center of the map and, using a colored pen, draw a line connecting each place to yourself.

You will need

A map of your home area

✳

A clock or watch

✳

Two pens, each a different color

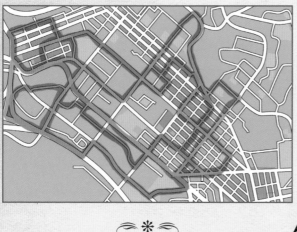

Now plot out the places associated with people or situations that you find difficult, or that cause anxiety in your life; use a different colored pen to connect yourself to these places. When the fifteen minutes are up, stop and gaze upon the drawing you have produced. Flashes of insight will occur; use these as a guide to help you deal with the challenges you face in your life.

For a spell to work, the spellcaster must be able to connect to the magical world. This connection can only be made when inner stillness is achieved.

⊰ ✳ ⊱

Walking the Hidden Paths

Witches and spellcasters accept the existence of "otherworlds," and know that these are the places where magic dwells. With the help of simple mental exercises, you can open up your mind and increase your sensitivity to these places. Such exercises require focus, patience, and practice, but they are necessary for most people who wish to connect to the magical world. Here is a simple exercise to put you in a magical state of mind.

METHOD

Make sure that you won't be disturbed for about thirty minutes. Light an incense stick and a candle, and sit upright in a chair, with your feet flat on the floor. Imagine the scent and light of the incense stick and candle enfolding you in silence and protection, forming an invisible sacred circle around you. Close your eyes and breathe slowly and deeply; concentrate on relaxing as you breathe out, and focus on the rhythm of your breathing as you breathe in.

You will need

**An incense stick
(any scent will do)**

✻

A candle

✻

Paper and a pen

Imagine yourself in your favorite outdoor location, until you feel you are really there. Feel the air, smell the scents, touch the ground, and hear whatever sounds are most pleasurable to you in that place. A sense of calm will soon envelop you, and a new magical world will come to open up before you. Open your eyes and jot down your impressions and feelings; these notes will help you achieve this sense of calm more quickly the next time you do this exercise.

CHAPTER 1

ELEMENTAL MAGIC

THE ELEMENTS OF EARTH, WATER, FIRE, AIR, AND
SPIRIT ARE USED AS A BASIS OF MOST FORMS OF MAGIC
AND RITUAL. THEY ARE OFTEN ASSOCIATED WITH THE
FOUR POINTS OF THE COMPASS, WITH SPIRIT AT THE
CENTER, ALTHOUGH DIFFERENT MAGICAL TRADITIONS
ALIGN THE ELEMENTS IN THEIR OWN WAYS. EACH OF
THE FOLLOWING SPELLS USES ELEMENTAL ENERGIES TO
BRING ABOUT A CHANGE IN AREAS OF YOUR LIFE, SO
MAKE SURE YOU ARE READY FOR THOSE CHANGES.

ANCIENT AND MODERN MAGIC WORKERS ALIKE STRESS
THE IMPORTANCE OF BALANCING THE ELEMENTS TO GIVE
POWER TO ANY SPELL WEAVING. THE ELEMENTS EACH
RELATE TO A DIFFERENT ASPECT OF LIFE. EARTH RELATES
TO THE MATERIAL WORLD AND PRACTICAL THINGS;
WATER TO EMOTIONS AND FEELINGS; FIRE TO ENERGY
AND ENTHUSIASM; AIR TO THE INTELLECT AND IDEAS;
AND SPIRIT TO THE INDWELLING POWER OF LIFE.

ELEMENTARY PRINCIPLES

Earth   Water   Fire   Air

REPRESENTING THE ELEMENTS

When working magic four of the elements are often placed at the edges of the magical circle to add their powers to the spells you weave. The following preparations help focus the mind and add energy to spells, but are not essential for the spells in this book.

Stones and pebbles represent the element earth.

EARTH: To represent the earth element, stones, earth, or even larger pieces of rock may be used.

WATER: The water element is best represented by liquid from a natural spring or well, or rainwater, but bottled mineral water may also be used.

Bottles of spring water symbolize the element water.

FIRE: Candles represent fire energy—and the force of the "divine light" that helps the wished-for magic come into effect. As long as they are housed in safe holders, any size or shape of candle may be used. Make sure candles are not positioned in a draft or where they can get knocked over, and if you burn them outdoors, put them in jars. The color of candle mentioned in the spells is important, but a white candle placed in a red holder or on a red plate makes a suitable substitute for a red candle, for example. Always snuff out candles before you leave the room.

Candles represent the element fire.

Incense represents the element air.

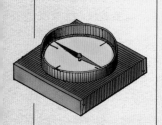

Use a compass to locate the four cardinal points: north, south, east, and west.

AIR: The idea of burning incense to symbolize the air element is very old, for it was thought that the power of prayer or spells could be carried upward in the smoke, to the realms of gods and angels. Incense can be found in many forms. Some edible herbs, such as rosemary, thyme, or basil, have stems that can be dried to make incense, and dried flowers of lavender, rose, or jasmine may also be used. Incense sticks and cones are available in many scents. Some people prefer to use aromatic oils and a burner because it does not give off any smoke. Whichever you choose, test the incense before using it in a spell, since some people react badly to particular scents by coughing or sneezing.

PREPARATION IS KEY

Prepare fully before attempting to weave a spell. You need to choose candles and other items with care. Clear a space, and set out any symbols you feel are necessary. Create a magical circle in space and time by placing symbols of the elements at the points of the compass (see The Spirit of Sacred Space, pages 38–39). This ritual helps you focus on the work ahead as it drives away distractions and unwanted energies.

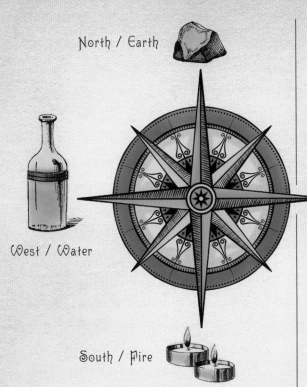

North / Earth

West / Water

East / Air

South / Fire

Place the symbols of the elements in the north, south, east, and west of your sacred space or altar.

THE ELEMENT OF SURPRISE

Magic does not always work in the way you expect, because it uses more than our familiar dimensions of time and space, so be prepared for surprises. However, anyone who has the perception to define an area of their current situation that could be improved will be able to use these spells and acts of magic to bring about beneficial transformations.

Magic is reliant upon the power of the elements, and earth is the first of these. Earth is the element of grounding and stability.

❧ ❋ ❧

The Spell of the Earth

MANY OF OUR GOALS AND AMBITIONS REQUIRE A FIRM, SOLID FOUNDATION IF THEY ARE TO BE COMPLETED SUCCESSFULLY. ANYTHING BUILT UPON AN UNSOUND BASE WILL ONLY COME CRUMBLING DOWN IN TIME. THIS IS NOT ONLY TRUE OF PROJECTS AT WORK OR AT HOME—IT IS ALSO TRUE OF RELATIONSHIPS OF ALL KINDS. THIS SPELL USES SYMBOLS REPRESENTING THE EARTH TO GIVE THE NECESSARY GROUNDING TO YOUR PROJECT OR RELATIONSHIP, PROVIDING A STABLE, FERTILE PLACE FOR IT TO GROW.

METHOD

Ideally this spell should be performed outdoors, but it will work indoors as well. Choose a project or a relationship that requires a strong foundation. Place a square piece of thick paper on the ground if outside, or on the floor if inside, and write down your objective using green, brown, or any earth-colored ink. Turn the paper over and, starting at the center, begin to draw a tight, clockwise spiral using the colored pen, until you reach the edge. As you draw, concentrate on your aim.

You will need

A square piece of thick paper

✳

A green, brown, or earth-colored pen

✳

Four pebbles or rocks taken from a natural setting, such as a garden, beach, or forest

✳

A bulb or large seed, such as an acorn, sunflower, or pumpkin seed

Place one stone on each corner of the paper, and put a bulb or large seed in the center of the spiral. Imagine the seed growing along the spiral path. If you are having trouble conjuring up this image, ask Mother Nature to assist you. Once you have set the magic in motion, remove the stones and the bulb or seed and bury them in the ground. Fold the paper into a small square, hide it in a safe place, and await a favorable outcome.

Emotions, which are traditionally symbolized by water, play an essential role in making magic happen.

≈ ✳ ≈

The MAGIC of WATER

In order for a spell to be successful, the emotions of the spellcaster must be open to receiving the energies of the spell. In other words, if you don't feel deeply about what you are trying to achieve when casting a spell, the spell will probably be unsuccessful. Water, which has long been associated with the emotions, can provide a means for you to connect to your deepest feelings, thereby opening yourself up to the power of the magic you are trying to access with the spell. By gazing into water, either contained in a bowl or in its natural environment, you can coax your emotions to the surface, and thus empower and enrich your magic.

METHOD

Spread a green or blue cloth on a table, and place a glass bowl in the center. Pour some water into the bowl. Dip two fingers into the water and recognize that much of your own body is comprised of water. Touch your forehead with your wet fingers, then flick a few drops to the north, south, east, and west. Sprinkle some flower petals upon the water and watch them float. Focus on something you have positive feelings about, like the love of your family. Feel the full strength of these emotions; do not worry if they make you cry. Then say:

"From the love in my heart, I send out love to the world."

After saying these words, you will feel a great release. Take the water outside and pour it into the ground.

You will need

A green or blue cloth

✳

A clear glass bowl

✳

Natural water from a spring, spa, rain, or the sea

✳

A compass

✳

A few flower petals

A spell to help you energize and empower every possible spell.

≈ ✳ ≈

The BEING of FIRE

WHETHER IN THE FORM OF A LIGHTED CANDLE, A BONFIRE, OR A HEARTH FIRE, THROUGHOUT HISTORY HUMANITY HAS RELIED UPON FIRE TO PROVIDE BOTH ENERGY AND LIGHT. IN THE REALM OF MAGIC, THE PERFORMANCE OF RITUALS IN DARKNESS LIT BY FIRELIGHT CAN ADD ENCHANTMENT TO THE WORK. MANY SPELLMAKERS USE REAL FIRE TO ENERGIZE THEIR SPELLS, BUT IT CAN BE JUST AS EFFECTIVE—AND SAFER—TO USE SOMETHING FLAME-COLORED INSTEAD, SUCH AS GOLDEN FLOWERS OR FABRIC, OR A LAMP WITH A CANDLE-SHAPED BULB. THIS SPELL CALLS UPON THE POWER OF FIRE TO BRING FORTH THE ENERGY TO CAST A SUCCESSFUL SPELL.

METHOD

Work this spell in a draft-free room. Put a
drop of scented oil on your finger and move
it up the length of the unlit candle, working
from the base toward the wick. Take care not
to get oil on the wick. Place the candle in
a secure holder and say:

≈ ✳ ≈

"Living light in candle flame,
let me give to you a name.
When I speak it be my friend,
and answer with a shake or bend.
I call you (give the flame a name)."

≈ ✳ ≈

Light the candle and, when the flame is steady,
speak to it, using the name you have chosen.
You may find that the flame sways
in response to the questions you
pose. When you have finished asking
your questions, thank the flame and
pinch it out. Save the candle for
the next time you wish to cast this
spell—the flame will speak again.

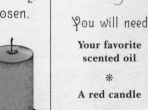

You will need

**Your favorite
scented oil**

✳

A red candle

A spell utilizing the clarity of air to help you find the solution to a problem.

◠ ✳ ◠

Air for INSPIRATION

Scents and incense have been used for thousands of years in religious and magical rituals. Whether in the form of incense sticks or cones, real incense grains burned on charcoal, or aromatherapy oils, a pleasant aroma can inspire clarity and enhance intuition and perception. Inextricably linked to the presence of an aroma is the act of breathing. When performing magic, rhythmic breathing can help develop the calmness and focus that are essential to spellmaking, especially if the air is pleasantly scented. Use this spell to summon forth the clarity of mind that you need to solve a problem that has been plaguing you.

METHOD

On a piece of paper, write down a problem you are currently facing. Place the paper underneath an incense burner containing your favorite scent. Now light the incense burner. Sit quietly, breathing deeply and slowly, and allow yourself to relax. Breathe in for a count of four, then hold for four, breathe out for four, and let your breath out for four. Repeat ten times. Count as fast or as slow as you need to, but always count evenly.

When you are done, think about a problem in your life, and strike the bell or metal object. On that note sing "help me" three times. Take a blue paper fan and gently waft the smoke from the burner away from you, watching the patterns it makes. A symbol of an answer will start to appear. Pass a feather through the smoke and carry it around with you until your problem has been solved.

You will need

Paper and a pen

✴

An incense burner

✴

**Your favorite
scented oil**

✴

**A small bell or metal
object that gives
off a clear note
when struck**

✴

**A small fan made of
folded blue paper**

✴

A feather

The element of the spirit is often symbolized by a lamp or a glass globe. To create a sacred space for working magic, it is necessary to find the spirit.

The Spirit of Sacred Space

USING ALL OF THE ELEMENTS—EARTH, WATER, FIRE, AIR, AND THE SPIRIT—THIS IS A SPELL TO HELP YOU TO CREATE A SAFE AND EFFECTIVE "SACRED SPACE," NOT JUST ON EARTH, BUT ALSO IN THE MAGICAL REALM, WHERE THE SPIRIT OF EFFECTIVE MAGIC CAN SURROUND YOU. WHEN YOU REACH SUCH A PLACE, YOUR INNER SENSES WILL OPEN UP AND YOUR SPELLS WILL BE EMPOWERED.

METHOD

Cover a small table in the center of your space with a green cloth. Using a compass, place the stone on the north side of the table; the water on the west; the lit candle on the south; and the lit incense sticks on the east. Place a glass sphere in the center. Imagine the strong Earth supporting you; the flowing waters of the oceans blessing you; the flame protecting you; the swirls of smoke inspiring you; and the sphere of the spirit enlightening you. Place your hand on the stone and say:

"I am a child of Earth, but my destiny lies beyond the starry heavens. I desire to enter the place beyond, to work magic for the good of all."

Give thanks and put aside the elemental symbols for the time being. A sacred space will have been created.

CHAPTER 2

The Power of the Planets

~ ✳ ~

THE EARLIEST WRITTEN SPELLS, GOING BACK
5,000 YEARS, DESCRIBE THE ENERGIES ATTRIBUTED
TO THE SEVEN ANCIENT PLANETS AND THEIR USE IN
MAGIC AND INCANTATIONS. EACH PLANET IS LINKED TO
PARTICULAR KINDS OF SPELL WEAVING, AND WHETHER
THEY ARE SEEN AS PERSONIFIED GODS AND GODDESSES,
OR SIMPLY DIFFERENT ENERGIES, EACH ONE CAN
HELP WITH A SPECIAL AREA OF OUR LIVES.

THE SUN, MASTER OF OUR SOLAR SYSTEM, FORMS A CENTER TO OUR MAGIC, THE MOON INSPIRES OUR VISIONS, MARS BRINGS ENERGY, MERCURY COMMUNICATES, VENUS OFFERS HARMONY, JUPITER GIVES CAREER ENHANCEMENT, AND SATURN TEACHES PATIENCE. THE MORE RECENTLY DISCOVERED PLANETS, URANUS, NEPTUNE, AND PLUTO, HELP WITH MODERN TECHNOLOGIES AND SKILLS.

CALLING on PLANETARY HELP

OLD AND NEW

The Sun, the Moon, Mercury, Venus, Mars, Jupiter, and Saturn have been observed for thousands of years and colors, numbers, metals, and influences attributed to each. Although not all these heavenly bodies are satellites of the Sun, from a magical point of view they are all called planets. Each of the "old" planets has an effect on different aspects of life and magic through the use of symbols. The "new" planets are also used, and their effects are felt in newer pursuits including information technology, the nuclear industry, space research, and the inner depths of psychology and mind power.

HEAVENLY INFLUENCES

Using the symbolism of each planet, including colors, scents, and flowers, in a spell to assist its related area of life can bring great personal benefits. Natural materials, like wood, plants, stones, or wool, work better than artificial substances. Threads used may be ordinary skeins of embroidery silk, or wool, or sewing thread braided into thicker strands. Ribbons may be narrow, wide, or simply strips cut from a piece of material.

Each of the old planets is associated with a day of the week. The Sun is linked with Sundays when his enlightening rays are

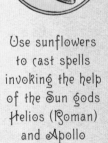

Use sunflowers to cast spells invoking the help of the Sun gods Helios (Roman) and Apollo (Greek).

Jasmine is sacred to the Moon goddesses Diana (Roman) and Artemis (Greek).

considered to be most magical, so Sunday is the most effective time to call upon his help. Monday is ruled by the psychic and visionary forces of the Moon. Tuesday comes under the protection of Mars, who helps with courage and determination. Wednesday is the domain of the great traveler, Mercury, and good for communication. Thursday is Jupiter's time, when commerce, career, and material growth can be helped. Venus rules Fridays, bringing harmony, joy, and love, and old Saturn, the grandfather of the planets, brings his slow and ancient wisdom to bear on Saturdays.

UNDERSTANDING THE MAGIC

I have been working with the powers of the planets for over forty years and found, through understanding their energies, often in conjunction with the goddesses and gods who share their names, that they really create change and bring wisdom. It is not necessary to believe in the ancient deities or to change your religious views to get spells to work, but to be open-minded, and accept that there are powers in the universe that can help us in our daily lives, is paramount. The power of each planet is indicated by the character of its namesake, a god or goddess of ancient civilizations, and each has something to offer the spellcaster as a filter of power and magic.

Although we know our Earth, with the other planets, orbits the Sun, and the Moon is the Earth's satellite, in astrology the Earth is seen as the center of the universe, with the Sun, Moon, and other planets circling it. Not only is the Earth the center, but you are the center too. From an esoteric point of view each person is the center of the cosmos, and from that still point can request help, guidance, or magical power from everything around. That help will be given, but there is always a price to pay, in terms of time and energy, dedication and respect, and eventually, thanksgiving for what is given.

Seek help related to travel by invoking Mercury (Roman) or Hermes (Greek) on a Wednesday.

Cast a spell on a Tuesday to ask for courage from Mars (Roman) or Ares (Greek).

A spell to enhance your self-confidence using the power of the Sun.

⮺ ✳ ⮺

The Sun: Inspiring Inner Strength

THE SOURCE OF LIFE ON EARTH AND AN IMPORTANT PART OF MYTHOLOGY, ART, AND LITERATURE, THE SUN IS SYMBOLIC OF OUR ABILITY TO DIRECT OUR WILL AND TO HAVE A SENSE OF PURPOSE. WITH THE HELP OF THE SUN'S LIGHT, YOU CAN INCREASE YOUR SELF-CONFIDENCE. THIS SPELL IS BEST PERFORMED ON A SUNDAY, WHEN THE SUN'S INFLUENCE IS STRONGEST.

METHOD

On a sunny day, take a lit gold candle and a glass of orange juice or any other golden-colored drink out into the sunshine (yellow and gold are sacred colors to the Sun). Hold the candle between your hands. Close your eyes and feel the warmth of the Sun shining on you. Sense the sunlight clearing away any self-doubt and disappointments. Now lift up the golden-colored drink and allow the sunlight to shine on it before drinking it. Say:

You will need

A sunny day

*

A gold candle

*

A glass of orange juice, or any other golden-colored drink

"Power of Sun, force of light, make my future strong and bright."

As you say these words, feel a powerful surge of inner strength flowing into you. Keep the gold candle in your bedroom so that you will be able to use its magical light and power whenever you need encouragement in the future.

Drawing on the magic of the Moon, this spell will put you in touch with your psychic side.

≈ ✳ ≈

The MOON of MYSTERY

THE FACE OF THE MOON HAS FASCINATED
PEOPLE FOR THOUSANDS OF YEARS. SOME OF
THE EARLIEST WORKS OF ART ARE MOON-
SHAPED, WITH TWENTY-NINE NOTCHES
MARKING A LUNAR MONTH. THE MOON'S
CYCLICAL WAXING AND WANING POWER
INFLUENCES OUR DREAMS AND MOODS,
AND CAN ALSO AWAKEN OUR PSYCHIC SELVES,
WHETHER HER FULL WHITE FACE OR MERELY A
SLIM, SILVER CRESCENT IS VISIBLE. THIS SPELL
IS BEST PERFORMED ON A MONDAY, WHEN THE
MOON'S INFLUENCE IS MOST POWERFUL.

You will need

A bright, moonlit evening

✳

A bouquet of white flowers, including jasmine if possible

✳

A small round mirror

METHOD

When the Moon is waxing bright in the sky, place a small bouquet of scented white flowers (white is sacred to the Moon) and a small round mirror on a windowsill. If possible, include jasmine in the bouquet, as it is sacred to the Moon as well. Standing in front of the windowsill and looking out at the Moon, chant these ancient words:

"O Moon of night, keeper of mystery, and bright stars' friend, whose silver beams succeed the fires of day, O three-formed Moon, who knows my dream, come to me and awaken my inner sight. So may this be."

Breathe on the mirror to make a mist, letting the moonlight shine upon it. Soon you will see a face form in the mirror—perhaps your own, perhaps that of a guiding spirit. In either case, ask the face for insight, then give thanks three times.

A modern spell calling upon the powers of Mercury to ensure a safe, trouble-free journey.

Mercury: the Traveler

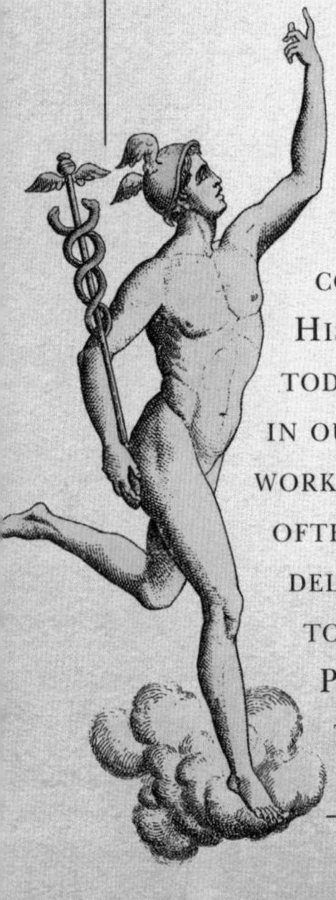

Mercury (as he is known in Roman mythology) or Hermes (Greek mythology) is the ancient god of communication and travel. His powers are much in demand today, as we travel a great deal in our modern world—both for work and for leisure—and we often run into problems and delays. This spell can be used to help avoid such difficulties. Perform it on a Wednesday, the day sacred to Mercury.

You will need

Sandalwood incense

*

An incense burner

*

A small wheel with spokes

*

Orange ribbon or thread

*

A piece of orange silk

METHOD

Place a small wheel with spokes and some orange ribbon or thread—orange is Mercury's magical color—on a table. Light some sandalwood incense (sandalwood is the aroma dedicated to Mercury) and pass the wheel through the smoke, saying: "Blowing air, have a care that I go safely everywhere." Now pass the ribbon through the smoke and begin to weave it through the wheel's spokes, saying:

⁓ ✳ ⁓

"Lord of travel, journeys' king,
keep me safe when traveling.
Guard my home when I'm away,
bring me safely back to stay.
Going forth and coming home,
be my watcher when I roam.
In the name of Mercury,
so may this be."

⁓ ✳ ⁓

Repeat the words three times, then wrap the wheel in a piece of orange silk. Carry it with you whenever you travel for a safe, trouble-free journey.

A spell to help you find true friendship or love.

✳

Venus: Lady of Love

Venus is the Roman mythological goddess of fertility, love, and pleasure (in Greek mythology she is known as Aphrodite). The great Roman emperor Julius Caesar claimed to be descended from her. Today, Venus remains a symbol of love and romance. Her symbols include the dove and roses; her day is Friday. She will not make anyone fall in love against their will, but her power can be used to help you recognize those qualities that make you lovable. By appreciating these qualities in yourself, you can increase your power to attract others—both friends and lovers.

METHOD

On a Friday at sunrise, thread six green buttons onto a piece of green cord or wool (green is the sacred color linked to Venus). Tie the ends of the cord or wool together to make a circle about 5 inches (13cm) across. Pull out a few of your hairs and tie them into the circle. Place the circle around the bottom of a vase of fresh roses, picked from your own garden if possible. Pour a drop of rose-scented oil onto your hand, sniff it, and say:

You will need

Six green buttons

*

Green cord or wool

*

Fresh roses in a vase

*

Rose-scented oil

"Lady of green, from high above,
send to me the power to love.
With this circle here entire,
send to me on wings of fire,
a vision from a heart confined,
that to my worth 1 am not blind,
and so a true friend or love can 1 find."

Allow a sense of your own goodness to emerge.

A spell calling upon Mars, the planet of courage, to help overcome obstacles.

Mars: the All-Powerful

In Roman mythology, the planet Mars was associated with war, and thus great strength and courage was associated with this planet. This spell calls upon these attributes for help in overcoming personal obstacles, and can be used to end a conflict or to provide physical endurance.

You will need

Scarlet felt, red sewing thread, and a needle

✻

Five small iron nails

✻

Two red candles

✻

Incense burner and your favorite incense

✻

A pinch of tobacco

METHOD

Using scarlet felt and red thread, sew together a bag strong enough to hold five small iron nails. On a Tuesday (the day sacred to Mars), stand two unlit red candles side by side. Burn some incense, along with a pinch of tobacco (the plant sacred to Mars). Pass the nails one by one through the smoke, saying: "Lord of iron, strength of steel, let your force my conflict heal." Place the nails in the bag and sew it shut. Light the left-hand candle and say:

"Mars, empower me with your light,
keep my courage shining bright,
that I may attain my right."

Now light the right-hand candle and say:

"Mars, defend me with your might, give mental strength in any fight, that I fear naught by day or night. Be it so."

Hide the bag for five weeks.
Your courage will keep you strong.

A spell to help you shine in the workplace and advance your career.

❋

JUPITER: LORD of JUSTICE

IN ROMAN MYTHOLOGY, JUPITER IS THE FATHER OF ALL GODS (IN GREEK MYTHOLOGY HE IS CALLED ZEUS). HE IS ALSO THE KING OF HEAVEN AND EARTH, AND IS CHARGED WITH THE ADVANCEMENT OF THE SOLAR SYSTEM. IN ASTROLOGY, JUPITER RELATES TO VOCATIONAL SUCCESS, AND REPRESENTS GROWTH AND EXPANSION. THIS SPELL CAN BE USED TO GAIN JUPITER'S SUPPORT IF YOU ARE EXPERIENCING PROBLEMS AT WORK, OR IF YOU ARE SEEKING AN ADVANCEMENT. IT SHOULD BE CARRIED OUT ON A THURSDAY, JUPITER'S SACRED DAY.

METHOD

Take a square of royal blue paper (royal blue is sacred to Jupiter) and a pen with gold ink, and write down a wish related to your work. Sign your name. Turn the paper over and copy this magical talisman dedicated to Jupiter onto the back.

4	14	15	1
9	7	6	12
5	11	10	8
16	2	3	13

You will need

A square of royal blue paper

✳

A pen with gold ink

✳

Four royal blue candles in brass holders

✳

Cedar incense

✳

An incense burner

✳

Blue silk

Light four royal blue candles and place them in brass holders (brass is Jupiter's metal). Burn some cedar incense (the scent dedicated to Jupiter) and ask Jupiter for the help you need. Repeat this spell every Thursday for four weeks, and your wish will be granted. In the meantime, wrap the paper square in blue silk (to insulate its energy) and carry it with you.

A modern spell for time management, patience, and endurance.

SATURN: LORD of TIME

AN ANCIENT ROMAN DEITY, SATURN IS THE LORD OF TIME. HE CAN EMPOWER SPELLS INVOLVING TIME AND PATIENCE. IN MODERN LIFE, IT CAN SEEM LIKE THERE IS NEVER ENOUGH TIME TO DO ALL WE WISH TO DO. NOT ONLY IS OUR TIME LIMITED, BUT OUR PATIENCE OFTEN IS AS WELL. THIS SPELL WILL HELP YOU MANAGE YOUR TIME BETTER, AND WILL INCREASE YOUR PATIENCE, TOO. CAST IT ON A SATURDAY, WHEN SATURN'S INFLUENCE IS STRONGEST.

You will need

Narrow black ribbon

∗

A black pen

∗

White card

∗

A coin

∗

Scissors

∗

A wristwatch

METHOD

Use a black pen to trace the shape of a coin onto a piece of white card. The circle should be no larger than the back of your wristwatch. On one side of the circle, draw the numbers of a clock face, but don't draw the hands. Cut out the circle and put it aside. Wind a length of black ribbon around your watch strap and say:

"Mighty Saturn, lord of time,
now I ask you hear my plea.
Let me learn to use the hours
of the day most usefully.
Break the bonds that tie me down,
teach me patience, day by day.
May your eyes of darkest brown
smile on me along my way.

✳

Repeat this mantra twice, then unwind and discard the ribbon. Affix the "timeless" clock face to the back of your wristwatch and wear it every day, until the paper falls away or tears. The spell should take effect within the month.

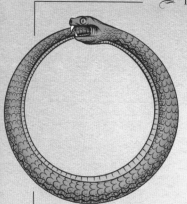

A planet of sudden transformation, Uranus's influence can be called upon for a quick, decisive outcome.

※

URANUS: the INNOVATOR

FIRST DISCOVERED BY WILLIAM HERSCHEL IN 1781, URANUS IS NAMED FOR THE GREEK GOD OF THE HEAVENS. ITS MAGICAL EFFECTS ARE LINKED TO ELECTRONICS, THE NUCLEAR INDUSTRY (WHICH USES URANIUM), INVENTIONS, AND NEW SCIENTIFIC DISCOVERIES. THE POWER OF URANUS CAN BE CALLED UPON TO PROTECT ELECTRONIC EQUIPMENT SUCH AS COMPUTERS, TABLETS, MUSIC PLAYERS, CELLPHONES, AND TELEVISIONS FROM POWER FAILURE, VIRUSES, AND OTHER PROBLEMS.

You will need

Thin card

❋

A pencil

❋

Glue

❋

Double-sided tape

❋

Silver foil

❋

Scissors

❋

A safe sparkler firework and something to light it with

METHOD

Gather together all the electronic equipment that you wish to protect. Draw the design of the Ourobouros, a snake with its tail in its mouth, on some card as many times as you have items to protect. Glue some silver foil onto the other side of the card and carefully cut out each snake symbol. Arrange the pieces of card in a circle, then light a sparkler. Draw a serpent in the air with the sparkler above each of the symbols, and ask Uranus, in your own words, to bless and protect all of your electronic equipment. When the sparkler has gone out, using double-sided tape stick the snake symbols onto the back of each item to be protected, placing them so they cannot be seen. Do not tell anyone that you have performed this spell or it will not work.

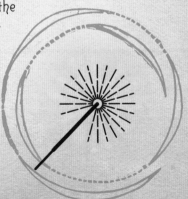

A spell calling upon the power of the distant planet Neptune to awaken your psychic visionary sense.

NEPTUNE: BRINGER of SIGHT

IN ROMAN MYTHOLOGY, THE GOD NEPTUNE RULES THE SEAS, ALL OF THE CREATURES WITHIN THEM, AND THE TIDES (IN GREEK MYTHOLOGY HE IS CALLED POSEIDON). WITH THE HELP OF HIS SUBTLE ENERGIES, YOU CAN USE THIS SPELL TO ACTIVATE YOUR HIDDEN PSYCHIC ABILITIES. THIS FORCE NEEDS TO BE CAREFULLY CONTROLLED, HOWEVER, SO THAT, LIKE A LARGE WAVE, IT DOES NOT OVERWHELM YOU.

METHOD

Place a glass bowl of water in front of you and add a few pinches of salt. If you have a real seashell, place it in the water. Now say:

"Become as the great sea, realm of Neptune, cradle of life. As your water is clear, so may my vision be clear."

You will need

A seashell (optional)

*

A clear glass bowl of water

*

Table salt

Sit quietly with your eyes closed. Breathe deeply and slowly. Breathe in for a count of four, hold it for four, then breathe out for four and hold for four. Repeat this exercise ten times. Imagine that your feet and legs are black, linking you to the Earth, and that your lap is scarlet, your belly orange, your solar plexus yellow, and your heart region green. See your throat as blue, your forehead as purple, and above your head, linking you to Heaven, a ball of brilliant white or violet fire. With this image in your mind, gaze into the water. If you are sufficiently relaxed and attuned, Neptune will grant you a vision.

A spell to summon forth the ancient power of Pluto to convene with your ancestors.

PLUTO: KEEPER of MEMORIES

THE PLANET PLUTO WAS NAMED AFTER THE ROMAN GOD OF THE UNDERWORLD (ALSO CALLED PLUTO). THE MYTHICAL UNDERWORLD IS OFTEN ASSOCIATED WITH A PSYCHOLOGICAL PHENOMENON KNOWN AS THE COLLECTIVE UNCONSCIOUS, WHERE ANCIENT ANCESTRAL MEMORIES ARE STORED. THIS SPELL CALLS UPON PLUTO'S POWER TO CONNECT YOU WITH YOUR ANCESTORS. PERFORM THIS SPELL AT NIGHT.

METHOD

Place a mirror on a stand, light a white candle, and place them both on a table, so that the light shines onto the mirror. Lay your family tree, or some other memento from your past, on the table and burn some incense.

Write on a piece of paper:

You will need

A mirror on a stand

✳

A white candle

✳

A copy of your family tree or other memento of the past

✳

Sweet, smoky incense and an incense burner

✳

Paper and a pen

"I wish to remember my ancestors, and those from my family who I have forgotten about. Reveal to me in this shining glass, I summon kind memories of my old family."

Carefully burn the paper in the candle flame, focusing your vision on the smoke reflected in the mirror. A face may appear in the mirror. When the image has faded, say: "Thank you, whoever you seem, perhaps we will meet again in a dream." You may meet a family member or an ancestor in your dreams.

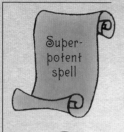

Super-potent spell

You will need

(Select materials related to your chosen planet)

✳

Colored candles

✳

Colored paper

✳

Colored silk

✳

Scissors

✳

A felt-tipped pen

✳

A small metal object

A talisman to bring you the luck of the planets.

✳

A Cosmos Spell

EACH PLANET RULES OVER ITS OWN SPECIAL DOMAIN, AND THUS EACH CAN BE ASKED FOR HELP IN A DIFFERENT AREA. ANCIENT TALISMANS WERE TYPICALLY WRITTEN ON ANIMAL SKINS USING SPECIAL INKS, OR WERE MADE OF METAL AND JEWELS, BUT MODERN ONES CAN BE MADE USING COLORED PAPER AND FELT-TIPPED PENS. OPPOSITE, YOU WILL FIND A LIST OF THE PLANETS, ALONG WITH THEIR ASSOCIATED POWERS, COLORS, METALS, NUMBERS, AND DAYS OF THE WEEK. DECIDE WHICH PLANET BEST REPRESENTS THE LUCK YOU NEED AND SUMMON IT FORTH WITH THE HELP OF THIS SPELL.

METHOD

On your chosen planet's day, collect
the appropriate number of candles,
some paper, a pen, and a piece of silk,
all in the planet's color. Find something
made of the metal dedicated to the
planet. Cut the paper into a shape with

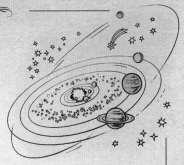

the appropriate number of sides, then write down the luck you
need. Light the candles, place the metal object on the paper, and
visualize yourself getting the help you need. Snuff out the candles
and wrap the paper in the silk, to protect its energy. Carry this
package around for two weeks. Your luck will come.

ANCIENT PLANET	DAY	METAL	COLOR	NUMBER	POWER
Sun	Sunday	Gold	Yellow	6	Health
Moon	Monday	Silver	White/Violet	9	Psychic skills
Mars	Tuesday	Iron	Red	5	Courage
Mercury	Wednesday	Quicksilver	Orange	8	Communication
Jupiter	Thursday	Tin	Blue	4	Expansion
Venus	Friday	Copper	Green	7	Harmony
Saturn	Saturday	Lead	Black	3	Patience

CHAPTER 3

The Magic of Time

❋

MOST PEOPLE KNOW WHICH SIGN OF THE ZODIAC
THEIR BIRTHDAY FALLS UNDER, BUT MAY NOT REALIZE
THAT, AS THE SUN MOVES ON ITS YEARLY JOURNEY
THROUGH THESE SIGNS, CERTAIN FORCES COME INTO
OPERATION. OUR EARLIEST ANCESTORS MAPPED OUT
THESE PERIODS OF TIME AND THE ENERGIES, BENEFITS,
AND DIFFICULTIES EACH OFFERED. AS EACH SIGN OF THE
ZODIAC RULES THE SKIES, ANYONE WHO WISHES MAY
MAKE USE OF THESE FORCES IN THEIR OWN LIVES.

MUCH MAGIC IS CONCERNED WITH TIME, CHOOSING THE RIGHT HOUR, DAY, MONTH, OR SEASON TO BRING ABOUT SPECIAL FORMS OF LUCK, PROGRESS, SELF-ASSURANCE, OR SUCCESS. MAGIC WORKERS ASSOCIATE CERTAIN KINDS OF SPELLS WITH PARTICULAR TIMES OF THE YEAR.

TIME'S INFLUENCE on MAGIC

THE ZODIAC TIMEPIECE

The signs of the zodiac form a circular wall of stars, with the Earth at the center. The exact movements of the planets within the signs of the zodiac are recorded in tables called Ephemeris, either in a book or on the internet. The constellations of the zodiac can be seen as numbers on the face of a great cosmic clock. Unlike our time clocks, the zodiac clock has one hand for each planet, moving at different speeds around the dial. In a person's horoscope, the settings of all these hands is recorded at the moment of birth, when the position of every sign and planet has a significance.

Our birthplace forms the central point around which these many influences move, faster or slower, throughout our lives, influencing everything we do.

To use the zodiacal influences in magic, we only need to weave spells that call upon each of the sign's specific powers. For simple spells you need to know when each sign of the zodiac has its greatest influence. Because of the wobble of the Earth against the stars, exact dates may vary from year to year, by a day or two (you can find this astrological information on the internet).

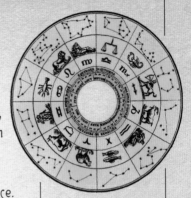

The constellations and zodiac signs form a cosmic clock around us.

Aries	March 21 to April 19	
Taurus	April 20 to May 20	
Gemini	May 21 to June 21	summer solstice
Cancer	June 22 to July 22	
Leo	July 23 to August 22	
Virgo	August 23 to September 22	autumn equinox
Libra	September 23 to October 22	
Scorpio	October 23 to November 21	
Sagittarius	November 22 to December 21	winter solstice
Capricorn	December 22 to January 19	
Aquarius	January 20 to February 18	
Pisces	February 19 to March 20	spring equinox

The ancient
Egyptians
associated
deities with the
constellations,
such as Osiris
with Orion and
Isis with Sirius.

SYMBOLS IN THE STARS

Records of certain fixed patterns of stars,
called constellations, were observed and named
by the wise peoples in many lands, especially
those with dry climates, where the skies are
usually clear for most of the year. In each
land these constellations were seen as vast
figures of people or things, and given names.
Stories were told about the great heroes of
the zodiac, Castor and Pollux, the twins of
Gemini, Leo the lion, or Sagittarius the
celestial archer. No one knows which came
first, the myth or the huge starry figures'
adventures. Sometimes, the heroine of an
old tale fell in love with an immortal god
and, as a gift, was given eternal life and
turned into a star. In ancient Egypt the god
Osiris is shown by the constellation we know
as Orion, and Isis, his wife, is shown by
Sirius, the brightest star in the sky, which
follows on the heels of Orion.

Early astronomers believed that children
born when certain stars were visible grew
up to show particular qualities. More recent
research by Michel Gauqueline, looking at the
horoscopes of soldiers, artists, doctors, and
sports figures, found that the position of
certain planets in their charts were similar.

The following zodiac spells can be used for
many purposes, in order to bring balance in a

relationship or justice to the world, or protection to a place or person, for example. The chart on pages 10–11 describes which zodiac signs are powerful on each day of the week. If you live in the southern hemisphere the zodiac signs from Gemini to Virgo are in the winter, so you will need to take this into account when spell weaving. If roses don't grow in your garden, then use another flower that you consider to be beautiful or that has a pleasing scent. However, some spells do relate to symbols of ancient traditions and these should never be mixed up, as this causes confusion to you and will cause the spell to fail.

Early astronomers believed that the positions of the stars at the time and place of your birth influence your character.

Grow plants associated with a particular zodiac sign to use in spell weaving.

Using the powers of Aries, a symbol of leadership, this is a spell for increasing assertiveness and self-confidence.

≈ ✳ ≈

ARIES: the RAM

A FIRE SIGN, ARIES IS BURSTING WITH DYNAMIC ENERGY. THIS SIGN USES INSPIRATION AS A CATALYST FOR CHANGE, AND ENCOURAGES FORWARD MOVEMENT. RULED BY THE RAM, ARIES ENERGY IS AGGRESSIVE AND COMPETITIVE, AS WELL AS EXCEEDINGLY CONFIDENT. USE THIS SPELL IF YOU LACK THE COURAGE AND STRENGTH TO GET WHAT YOU WANT.

You will need

A red candle

❋

A picture of a ram

❋

A red flower

❋

A compass

❋

A sheet of
white paper

❋

A red pen

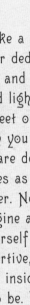

METHOD

Take a red candle, a red flower (red is the color dedicated to Aries), and a picture of a ram and place them on a table. Face the east and light the candle. Using a red pen, on a sheet of white paper list the situations in which you wish you were more assertive. When you are done, carefully fold the paper as many times as you can and place it underneath the flower. Now sit still with your eyes closed and imagine a warm red light shining on you. See yourself becoming stronger willed and more assertive, yet not vicious or cruel. Know deep down inside that you can be strong if you need to be. Pinch out the candle, but leave the folded paper underneath the flower until the flower has dried out completely. The next time you are facing a difficult situation, recall the warmth of the red light.

A spell to open your eyes and help you appreciate the beauty in your life.

TAURUS: the BULL

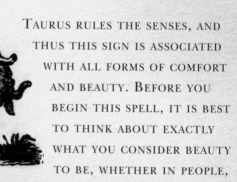

TAURUS RULES THE SENSES, AND THUS THIS SIGN IS ASSOCIATED WITH ALL FORMS OF COMFORT AND BEAUTY. BEFORE YOU BEGIN THIS SPELL, IT IS BEST TO THINK ABOUT EXACTLY WHAT YOU CONSIDER BEAUTY TO BE, WHETHER IN PEOPLE, WORKS OF ART, OR THE NATURAL WORLD; AS THE OLD SAYING GOES, "BEAUTY IS IN THE EYE OF THE BEHOLDER." IF YOU LOOK HARD ENOUGH, YOU WILL FIND THAT THERE IS BEAUTY IN ALL OF THE PEOPLE, OBJECTS, AND EVENTS IN YOUR LIFE, HOWEVER ORDINARY THEY MAY SEEM. HERE IS A SPELL TO OPEN YOUR EYES TO THIS BEAUTY AND TO HELP YOU APPRECIATE IT.

METHOD

Set out onto a table a collection of things that you love; you can include your favorite flowers, pictures of the people you love, your favorite objects—anything in your life that makes you happy. Also include a few ribbons in your favorite colors. Stand facing south, hold your hands over the objects, and say:

You will need

Your favorite objects

✳

Pictures of the people you love

✳

Ribbons in your favorite colors

✳

A compass

"May 1 have beauty before me. May 1 have beauty behind me. May 1 have beauty to my left hand and to my right hand. May 1 have beauty all about me, and may 1 walk in beauty through my whole life, through this beautiful world."

◈ ✳ ◈

Tie three knots in each of the ribbons and carry them around with you. You will soon recognize and appreciate the beauty in all that surrounds you.

A spell for renewing communication with a long-lost friend, relative, or lover.

GEMINI: the TWINS

GEMINI IS RULED BY MERCURY, THE PLANET OF TRAVEL AND COMMUNICATION. THIS SIGN IS CONCERNED WITH IDEAS, CHANGE, AND PERSONAL COMMUNICATIONS. GEMINI'S SYMBOL IS II, THE ROMAN NUMERAL FOR TWO. ACCORDINGLY, ITS POWER MAY BE USED TO RECONNECT TWO FRIENDS, RELATIVES, OR LOVERS WHO HAVE LOST TOUCH WITH EACH OTHER.

You will need

Mementos of the person

✻

A photograph of yourself and one of the person

✻

A large envelope to hold the photos

✻

Orange ribbon

✻

Adhesive tape

METHOD

Sit quietly and consider your relationship with the missing person. Place mementos of the person around you, and recall when you last saw or spoke to each other. Place a photo of yourself and one of the loved one face to face inside an envelope and seal it shut. Bind the envelope with orange ribbon, reciting:

"With ribbon I bind this symbol to find my ____(friend, relative, or lover) from time gone by. Saying that he (or she) shall remember me, and a message swiftly fly, to unite us from the Earth's ends, together by day or night."

Tape the envelope to a window in your home, facing the direction the long-lost person is in, and mentally send out your address or phone number to them. Within two weeks, a message—often via a strange route—will bring news of them. Take down the envelope and unwind the ribbon to release the spell, thanking Gemini.

A spell to create a tough shell to protect and defend a vulnerable interior.

CANCER: the CRAB

CANCER IS SYMBOLIZED BY A CRAB WITH A HARD SHELL—TENDER UNDERNEATH, YET TOUGH ON THE OUTSIDE. ALTHOUGH PEOPLE BORN AT THIS TIME ARE BY NATURE SOFT-HEARTED, SENSITIVE, AND COMPASSIONATE, THEY, LIKE MOST OF US, CAN AT TIMES BENEFIT FROM THE ABILITY TO PROJECT AN ARMOR-PLATED EXTERIOR TO THE WORLD. WHEN YOU ARE FEELING VULNERABLE, THIS SPELL CAN HELP YOU BUILD A PROTECTIVE SHELL TO NESTLE INTO UNTIL YOU FEEL STRONG AGAIN.

You will need

A small box with a separate lid

Aqua, blue, or green paper

❋

Glue

❋

Scissors

❋

A seashell

❋

Silver string

METHOD

Take a small box with a separate lid and cover both parts with green, blue, or aqua-colored paper (symbolizing the water the crab comes from). Snip off a few strands of your hair, place them and a seashell in the box, and put the lid on. Take some silver string and wind it around the box while saying:

≈ ✳ ≈

"As I wind this string to bind,
a box of protection making.
I will be strong as I go along,
my heart is not for breaking.
Should I fear, in any year,
this charm I shall remember,
and know its power, in every hour,
from January to December."

≈ ✳ ≈

Hide the box on top of a cupboard or some other high place. You will soon find it much easier to cope with difficult people and situations.

A spell to give you confidence
and to enhance your position
in the eyes of others.

LEO: the LION

THE ANCIENT GREEK GOD HERACLES'S FIRST
LABOR WAS TO KILL THE NEMEAN LION, AND
THE CONSTELLATION LEO IS SAID TO HONOR
THE BRAVERY OF THIS BATTLE. BUT DESPITE
THE VIGOR AND STAMINA ATTRIBUTED TO THIS
MYTHICAL LION, LIONS IN THE REAL WORLD ARE
KNOWN TO BE RATHER LAZY, SPENDING A LOT OF
TIME EATING, RESTING, PLAYING, OR GROOMING
THEMSELVES. THIS SPELL IS FOR THOSE WHO
DESIRE THE POSITIVE "LIONLIKE" QUALITIES,
BUT ARE NOT KEEN
ON DOING ANYTHING
TOO STRENUOUS TO
ACQUIRE THEM.

You will need

Metallic gold paper

✳

Scissors

✳

A pen

✳

**Six yellow flowers,
such as marigolds,
sunflowers, and
yellow daisies**

✳

A shallow bowl

✳

A gold chain

✳

**Gold-colored
baubles**

✳

A tea light

METHOD

Cut out a circle of metallic gold paper. Write your name on it and draw the symbol for the astrological sign Leo.

Take the paper outdoors on a sunny day and place it where the Sun can shine upon it. Lay the petals of six yellow or gold-colored flowers outside to dry out in the Sun. When the petals are dry, place them in a shallow bowl with a gold chain, some gold-colored baubles, and a tea light. Set the bowl on top of your golden circle and light the tea light. See the tea light's flame reflected on the golden objects and say:

❋

"I shall shine,
be strong as a lion,
my way ahead is bright.
My heart is gold,
its power unfolds to show
my own true light.
May I shine, may I shine,
in everything I do."

❋

Place the golden circle on the floor underneath the head of your bed. Wear the chain whenever you are going to face a challenging situation, and know that you will succeed.

A harvest spell to help you reap the fruits of your efforts.

❊

VIRGO: the VIRGIN

You will need

Fruits, grains, seeds, berries, flowers, twigs, autumn leaves (found, not bought)

❊

Symbols of completed projects, or of those that you wish to discard

❊

Photos of your family and friends

❊

Paper and a pen

❊

A candle

❊

String

THE CONSTELLATION VIRGO IS LINKED TO DEMETER, THE GREEK GODDESS OF THE HARVEST. AS IN ANCIENT TIMES, TODAY THE COMING OF WINTER IS A GOOD TIME FOR HARVESTING THE REWARDS OF YOUR ACHIEVEMENTS FOR THE YEAR, AND FOR DISCARDING THAT WHICH IS NO LONGER NECESSARY IN YOUR LIFE. BY HARVESTING THE FRUITS OF YOUR LABOR, YOU CAN GATHER THE BENEFICIAL ENERGIES THAT WILL SUSTAIN YOU FOR THE REST OF THE YEAR.

METHOD

Collect flowers, fruits, seeds, berries, twigs, leaves, and anything harvested from your own garden. Gather as well some symbols of your work—in particular, anything that symbolizes projects that you have completed, or that you wish to discard. Finally, gather some photos of your family and friends. On a warm afternoon, set up a table and make a sacred space around it (see pages 38–39), then set out all of the objects that you have gathered. Burn any paper symbols of completed or discarded projects using the flame of a candle, then say:

"Mother Nature, who has given me a bounty, you who inspires my work, nourishes me, body and spirit, I give thanks for all that you have granted me. With these tokens I offer myself to protect the Earth."

Tie the "natural" symbols into a bundle with a string and hang it on the branch of a tree. Place the photos where you can see them at home or work, until Yuletide.

A spell for balance, and to help you make the right decisions in your life.

⇒ ✳ ⇐

LIBRA: the SCALES

You will need

Paper and a pen

✳

A small pendulum (you can make this by suspending a weight on a piece of thin string)

✳

A black candle and a white candle

✳

An image of the Scales of Justice

✳

A compass

THE CONSTELLATION LIBRA IS ASSOCIATED WITH BALANCE AND JUSTICE. IN OUR DAILY LIVES, WE OFTEN HAVE TO JUGGLE CONFLICTING DEMANDS ON OUR TIME AND ENERGY, AND IT CAN BE DIFFICULT TO KNOW HOW TO BALANCE THESE DEMANDS. WHEN YOU FEEL YOU NEED HELP PRIORITIZING THE MANY OBLIGATIONS IN YOUR LIFE, USE THIS SPELL TO CALL UPON THE WISDOM OF LIBRA.

METHOD

Think about the demands on your time and write on a
piece of paper: "Should 1 choose (choice A) or (choice B)?"
Take a small pendulum and hold it over your right palm.
Ask it: "Can you show me a yes?" Note how it swings, then
say: "Can you show me a no?" The pendulum will now
swing differently. Light a black and a white candle
and place the paper between them. Now place a picture
of the Scales of Justice in front of the paper.
Holding your pendulum over the paper, say:

"Power of the pendulum, answer me,
should 1 select choice A or B?
Is it right to make my way
along the path that follows A?
Would a better option be
if 1 go along with B?"

Then say: "Is A the right path?" If the pendulum signals that the
answer is no, then say: "Is B the right path?" You must abide by
the decision shown to you by the pendulum. Stick the picture of
the Scales of Justice on the eastern wall of your bedroom and
leave it there until the project is completed.

A spell to summon forth the identity of your secret admirer.

~ * ~

Scorpio: the Scorpion

AT THE HEART OF THE SCORPIO CONSTELLATION IS THE BRIGHT RED STAR ANTARES, WHICH BURNS WITH AN INTENSE ENERGY AND CORRESPONDS TO THE PURPOSEFUL AND PASSIONATE NATURE OF THOSE WHO ARE BORN DURING THIS TIME. HERE IS A SPELL THAT UTILIZES THE PASSIONATE ENERGY OF SCORPIO TO UNCOVER THE IDENTITY OF A SECRET ADMIRER.

You will need

Paper and a pen

✳

Four candles of your favorite color

✳

A small mirror

✳

A new silver ring

✳

Your favorite incense

✳

Incense burner

METHOD

On a piece of paper, write down what you want from a lover, and what you are willing to give in return. Then set four candles of your favorite color in a square. Place a small mirror in the center of the square, and place a new silver ring upon the mirror (silver, the metal of the Moon, represents the emotions). Light the candles and your favorite incense and think about what you have written. Look into the mirror through the ring and say:

"Scorpion, power of love,
send an image from above,
if there is one who truly loves me,
let me now their picture see.
If this secret can't be told,
let my love shine out like gold,
that a love may come, soon."

The face of your secret admirer may now appear in the mirror. Whether or not it does, kiss the ring and slip it on your finger. Any secret admirers will soon make themselves known.

A charm enlisting the talents and skills of the Archer to help bring success in sport.

SAGITTARIUS: the ARCHER

THE SYMBOL OF SAGITTARIUS IS A MOUNTED ARCHER. THOSE BORN AT THIS TIME OF THE YEAR ARE INCLINED TOWARD A DESIRE FOR PERSONAL FREEDOM, RESTLESSNESS, AND A LOVE OF THE OUTDOORS. THEY OFTEN HAVE AN INTEREST IN SPORTS, AND ENJOY BOTH SOLITARY SPORTING ACTIVITIES AND PLAYING AS PART OF A TEAM. HERE IS A CHARM CALLING UPON THE SPORTING PROWESS OF SAGITTARIUS TO BRING SUCCESS IN A SPORTING ENDEAVOR.

You will need

A photo of the prize you seek

✳

Thread, wool, or thin ribbon in red, blue, white, black, and green

✳

Five metal rings

✳

Paper and a pen

✳

A small red cloth pouch

METHOD

Ideally you should dress in your sporting costume while working this magic. Place a picture of the prize you seek in front of you. Tie a different-colored thread to each of five metal rings, saying:

— ✳ —

"May my dedication take me higher,
to win the prize I so desire.
When the race is run so fast
may I be nearer first not last.
Hard training will make me stronger,
so I can go on much longer.
With my team I'll be a part,
sharing my skills with all my heart.
As I strive to win the gold,
sportsmanship I will uphold."

— ✳ —

Repeat this mantra five times. Neatly write out a copy of the spell, and place it, along with the rings and the photo of the prize you seek, in a red pouch. Keep the pouch near you whenever you play the sport and your skill will improve.

A garland spell for security and success in your career.

CAPRICORN: the GOAT

IN MANY ANCIENT CULTURES, MIDWINTER, OR THE WINTER SOLSTICE, WAS A TIME FOR CELEBRATING THE PREVIOUS TWELVE MONTHS, AND FOR MAKING PLANS FOR THE COMING YEAR. WITH THIS SPELL, YOU BUILD UPON THIS TRADITION BY MAKING A GARLAND THAT INCORPORATES SYMBOLS OF YOUR ACHIEVEMENTS FROM THE PREVIOUS YEAR, TO GIVE YOU THE STRENGTH AND CONFIDENCE YOU WILL NEED TO FACE CHALLENGES IN THE YEAR TO COME.

METHOD

Begin by making a small garland of greenery, about 1 foot (30cm) or less across, using holly, ivy, spruce—the plants dedicated to Capricorn—and any other greenery you can find. Bind it with florist's wire. Add symbols of your job to the garland, such as photos or small parts of projects you have finished. Take some green ribbon and wind it clockwise around the garland, then take some dark blue ribbon and wind it counterclockwise around the garland, joining the ends in a bow. In the middle of the garland, hang strands of gold thread, coins, beads, and tinsel. When your garland is complete, light a rose, a cedar, and a myrrh incense stick and wave the garland through the smoke of each, picturing success and security at work in the year to come. Say:

You will need

Holly, ivy, spruce, and other available greenery

✳

Florist's wire

✳

Symbols of your job

✳

Green and dark blue ribbons

✳

Gold thread, beads, and tinsel

✳

Real or chocolate gold-colored coins

✳

Rose, cedar, and myrrh incense

"I ask for success and security, it is my will. So may it be."

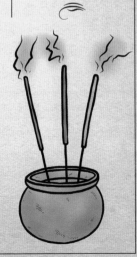

Hide the garland in a dark place, knowing it will bring you success in your career in the coming year.

A benevolent spell for helping people in need and charitable causes.

≈ ✳ ≈

AQUARIUS: the WATER CARRIER

SOME ASTROLOGERS BELIEVE THAT THE YEAR 2000 MARKED THE
MOVEMENT OF THE SPRING EQUINOX TO THE CONSTELLATION
AQUARIUS; THUS WE ARE ON THE CUSP OF THE AGE OF AQUARIUS.
THIS AGE WILL LAST 2000 YEARS, AND MANY BELIEVE THAT IT
WILL BE CHARACTERIZED BY PEACE AND HARMONY.
APTLY, THE SYMBOL FOR AQUARIUS IS A LONE
WATER BEARER, POURING THE WATERS OF LIFE
FOR OTHERS. WITH THIS SPELL, YOU CAN
HONOR THE BENEVOLENCE OF AQUARIUS
BY HELPING THE LESS FORTUNATE OR
BY FURTHERING A CAUSE DEVOTED
TO BETTERING THE PLANET.

METHOD

Choose a project or charity that you wish to help. Go to a nearby river, and take with you a bottle of spring water, a glass container, and a glass nugget or marble. Stand beside the river, holding the bottle in your hands, and wish as hard as you can that a solution to a desperate situation may be found. Pour half of the bottle of spring water into the river, and say:

You will need

A bottle of spring water

✳

A glass container

✳

A glass nugget or marble

"Every river connects to the sea, and every ocean connects to the others. Rain drawn from the sea falls on the land. All people are brothers. Let my intent travel around the whole world, reaching those in greatest need."

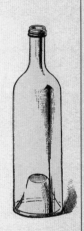

Kiss the glass nugget or marble and throw it into the river. Pour the rest of the spring water into the glass container and take it home. Set it in a place where you will see it often, and remember your good wish for the world.

A spell to give you the strength to achieve your most challenging aspirations and desires.

Pisces: the Fish

PISCES, THE TWELFTH SIGN OF THE ZODIAC, IS REPRESENTED BY TWO FISH SWIMMING IN OPPOSITE DIRECTIONS, BOUND TOGETHER BY A LINE. THIS IMAGE REPRESENTS A DUALITY, THE STRUGGLE OF THE SPIRITUAL SOUL WITHIN THE PHYSICAL BODY. IN THE CHINESE TRADITION OF FENG SHUI, FISH ARE OFTEN USED TO HELP STIR UP ENERGIES WHERE THERE IS A DEAD PLACE IN A HOUSE. IN THIS SPELL, THEY ARE USED TO STIR UP ENERGY AND INSPIRATION.

METHOD

Twist some stiff wire into a circle and tie pale blue, sea-green, and silver ribbons onto it. Cut out the shapes of two fish from gold-colored paper. Using silver thread, hang the fish and some small bells or wind chimes to the mobile, so that they swing freely. As you are creating this mobile, think of long-term plans that need to be set in motion, or about any aspirations or desires that seem especially difficult to accomplish.

Make the mobile as beautiful as you can. Look at the bells, ribbons, and fish, and see each as a symbol of energy and inspiration. With a red ribbon, hang the mobile in a corner of a room where a draft can stir it, keeping the ribbons and fish moving and allowing the bells or wind chimes to ring.

From time to time, light an incense stick and place it near the mobile, so that the scent wafts in the same breeze. Each time the mobile sways in the breeze, it will draw your hopes and desires for the future closer.

You will need

Stiff wire

✽

Pale blue, sea-green, and silver ribbons

✽

Gold-colored paper

✽

Scissors

✽

Small bells or wind chimes

✽

Silver thread

✽

Red ribbon

✽

Sweet-scented incense sticks

CHAPTER 4

KITCHEN WITCHING

❦ ✳ ❧

EVERYONE HAS A KITCHEN, AND IN ITS CABINETS
AND STORES THERE ARE NUMEROUS USEFUL ITEMS
THAT CAN BE USED TO BRING LUCK, HARMONY, AND
MANY OTHER BENEFITS TO THE MAGIC WORKER.
BY CAREFULLY CONSIDERING THE LUCK YOU NEED
AND EXPLORING THE HERBS, SPICES, DRIED FRUITS,
AND KITCHEN IMPLEMENTS AT HAND, YOU CAN
ENCHANT YOUR LIFE WITH THE TASTES AND
SCENTS OF DELICIOUS CHARMS.

THIS COLLECTION OF MAGICAL SPELLS USES COMMON PLANTS, HERBS, AND SPICES THAT YOU MAY ALREADY HAVE IN YOUR KITCHEN. IF YOU GROW THESE PLANTS YOU CAN USE FRESH LEAVES OR STEMS, BUT DRIED CULINARY HERBS WILL WORK AS WELL. PLANTS CAN BE USED AS TALISMANS AND LUCK-BRINGERS, IN HEALING AND SOOTHING TEAS, AND TO WARD OFF HARM.

MAGIC from of the HEART the HOME

A SPELL WEAVER'S STOREROOM

The kitchen is traditionally the heart of the house, where the daily benediction of preparing food takes place. It is where many of the original tools of the witch or spellmaker are to be found, including the besom, the old-fashioned broom made of birch bristles bound

The kitchen is
a treasure trove
of magical tools
and ingredients.

Use a broom to
sweep a symbolic
magical circle for
spellcasting.

to a handle of sacred ash. The cups and bowls
are all used in various forms of spells and
charms, saucepans have replaced the cauldron
in which potions are brewed, and teapots
make herbal tisanes. Spices, found in most
kitchen cabinets, have particular attributes
for bringing health and wisdom, pleasure
and protection to those who use them. In fact,
most herbs and spices that are safe to eat, in
appropriate portions, are safe to use in magic.

THE KITCHEN TRADITION

In the past, many herbs and useful plants for
dyeing and magical purposes would be grown
or gathered from the wild, so a knowledge
of the names and natures of these was
very important. Much of this plant lore was
handed down through families, and in most
communities there were men and women who

Kitchen pans
and teapots are
the modern-day
witch's cauldron.

Witches, or wise women, grew plants and herbs for both medicine and magic.

possessed skills in using plants for medicine or herbs for healing. Later these people were called by other names, such as witches, wise women, or cunning men. They kept the magical arts alive, drawing on inherited wisdom to preserve and expand their knowledge of useful materials. When books began to circulate, first as handwritten manuscripts and later as printed works, witches expanded their knowledge using information from other lands and earlier times.

As well as using plant magic they understood the power of the seasons, knowing when it would be best to perform

any kind of magic, divination, or healing.
They observed everyone and everything that
happened around them, from the opening of
the first flower in spring to the migration
of birds, the movements of clouds, and the
activities of their neighbors. All this could
help them see into the future or give advice
to those who asked. They worked closely with
the powers of nature, with stones and twigs,
pure water, and dark skies studded with stars,
where they saw what was to be. Much of this
ancient knowledge has come down to us, but
we can only get it to work if we carefully
follow the rules, wishing harm to no one,
and seeking to change only ourselves.

MODERN-DAY MAGIC

The following spells are based on tried and
tested old arts, but they will work as well in
the twenty-first century as they did in the
twelfth, if those who seek to understand
old magic treat it with respect and care.
By carefully preparing for any spell, getting
all the necessary items, the threads, spices,
containers, and so on, ready before starting,
and preparing yourself, you can draw on the
great store of inherited wisdom and the vast
power of the gods of nature, to help with
your spells and bring you luck, just as your
ancestors did in days gone by.

Signs observed
in nature, such
as migrating
birds, have
been used for
divination since
ancient times.

A traditional spell using the herb mint to ask for greater riches.

MAKE a MINT

MINT IS A HERB USED IN TEA AND COOKING, BUT THE WORD ALSO DESCRIBES THE PLACE WHERE MONEY IS CREATED. BY USING THIS HERB IN A SPELL, YOU MAY ATTRACT A SMALL AMOUNT OF CASH TO YOURSELF. IF YOU REQUIRE MONEY IN ORDER TO BUY AN OBJECT OR ACCOMPLISH A TASK, A SPELL AIMED AT THIS END RESULT MAY BE MORE EFFECTIVE. HOWEVER, IF YOU JUST NEED A BIT OF EXTRA CASH TO GET YOU THROUGH THE WEEK, THIS SPELL CAN HELP.

You will need

Green felt

✳

Green thread and needle

✳

Ten whole dried mint leaves

✳

Sky blue paper and pen

✳

Four gold candles

✳

Four coins of different values

METHOD

Make a pouch of green felt (green symbolizes both the money and the mint) and place ten dried mint leaves inside. On a sheet of sky blue paper (to symbolize the riches that will materialize "from the heavens"), write a sum of money, preferably less than $100. Place the pouch on a table with the paper. Place one gold candle and one coin at each corner of a square and light the candles. Now sing, in any tune you like:

"Lord of money, this I pray,
that some cash will come my way.
I will work to earn the sum,
if to me it now will come,
and by effort I shall pay for
all the coins that come my way."

Dance around the candles four times, then sit quietly, holding the mint pouch, and consider whether a lottery win, a new job, or the payment of a debt owed to you would provide you with what you need. You may soon find yourself a bit wealthier.

A spell to open your mind to what has been forgotten.

≈ ✳ ≈

Rosemary
for
Remembrance

Rosemary is a wonderful herb that can be used in cooking, as a soothing tea, or as incense (hence its old French name, *incensier*). Bees love the blue flowers, and the leaves keep stored clothes smelling sweet. Traditionally it was thought to help the brain and memory; in *Hamlet*, Shakespeare wrote "There's rosemary, that's for remembrance…", and sprigs were often carried at funerals. Here is a charm you can make using the power of rosemary to improve your memory.

You will need

Four freshly picked sprigs of rosemary

✳

Pale blue, dark green, red, and white embroidery thread

✳

Green ribbon

METHOD

On a dry sunny day, pick four stems of rosemary, one by one, while saying:

✳

"This twig I pick that I may remember all my deeds from May to December. This twig I gather that I may recall all of my friends in the spring or the fall. These rosemary leaves I gently take to recall good times with no mistake. This stem I pluck from the green rosemary that my love will not forget me."

✳

Place the tips of two stems one way and the other two the opposite way. Bind the bundle with threads of pale blue (for the flowers), dark green (for the leaves), red (for the stems), and white (for the underside of the leaves), so you end up with a cigar-shaped charm. Tie a green ribbon around the middle of the charm and hang it where you will see it every day. Every time you see the charm, you will be reminded of the things you must not forget.

A spell for summoning the power of sage to increase your wisdom.

※

SAGE for WISDOM

IN THE MIDDLE AGES, THERE WAS A WELL-KNOWN SAYING: "IF YOU WOULD LIVE FOREVER AND AYE, EAT SOME SAGE LEAVES EVERY DAY." TRADITIONALLY, NATIVE AMERICANS USED DRIED SAGE, BOUND INTO BUNDLES AND SET SMOLDERING, TO PURIFY THEIR SACRED SPACES. BUT MOST OF ALL, SAGE HAS LONG BEEN KNOWN AS THE HERB FOR WISDOM. THE CELTS BELIEVED THAT IF A BRIDE CARRIED SAGE, SHE BECAME WISE. HERE IS A SPELL TO INCREASE YOUR ABILITY TO DRAW WISDOM FROM LIFE EXPERIENCE.

You will need

Nine freshly picked stems of sage

❋

The symbols of the four elements—a stone, a bowl of water, a red candle, and incense—placed around the edge of an altar (see The Spirit of Sacred Space, pages 38–39)

❋

If you do not have a garden, a plant pot with earth in it

METHOD

Pick nine stems of sage before the herb has flowered, when the Moon is waxing. Set up an altar using the four elemental symbols. Lay the sage twigs, all in the same direction, in a circle in the center of the altar. Light the elemental candle and sing:

"In magic circles of every age,
when wind is calm or tempests rage,
when magic sleeps or folly shows,
from this ring of holy sage,
let the power of wisdom flow."

Pick up one leaf and chew it, imagining it awakening insight, common sense, and wisdom within you. The other stems should be taken outside and planted in the ground, or in a plant pot. If they grow, wisdom will be yours for the rest of your life.

As we all know, time and tide wait for no man, so here is a spell to master time.

Take Back Thyme

In today's hectic world, many people are hard-pressed to find the time to do everything that needs to be done. Indeed, we often find that our time is not our own. This spell will help you restore some spare time to your life by setting a pattern during a week-long magical rite.

You will need

A pot of growing thyme, any variety

*

Silver foil

*

Paper and a pen

*

Sweet-scented oils

*

Candles

*

Black marker

METHOD

Choose a time frame of 15 minutes every day when no one will disturb you. On day one of seven, take a pot of thyme and cover it with silver foil (symbolizing mind power). Relax, breathing deeply for a few minutes. Make a list of the things you need time to do—these must be things just for you. Place the list under the thyme pot. On day two, take a bath with scented oils by candlelight and think about your list. Then add to the list and inspect the plant, watering it and giving it kind words. On day three, list things that waste your time. On day four, select a relaxing task from your first list and do it, stating:

⊰ ✳ ⊱

"This is my time, and be sure that I'm going to use it how I will. No other can my time slot fill."

⊰ ✳ ⊱

On day five, talk to your thyme plant, pouring out your complaints and delights. On day six, try something new that you have always wanted to try. On day seven, take the list of time-wasting items and cross out each one firmly with a black marker. Recognize that you can take back your life. Perform this ritual as often as needed for the rest of your life.

A household spell to clean up your kitchen and find a hidden treasure.

A Treasure Hunt

NOBODY LIKES TO DO KITCHEN CHORES, BUT WITH IMAGINATION AND SOME MAGIC, THEY CAN BE ENJOYABLE. HERE IS A SPELL FOR TIDYING UP AND FOR REVEALING A HIDDEN TREASURE AT THE SAME TIME. SEVERAL PLAYERS CAN PERFORM THIS SPELL TOGETHER. YOU CAN ALSO USE THIS SPELL IN OTHER ROOMS IN YOUR HOME.

You will need

An old sheet

✳

A messy drawer or cupboard

✳

New string

✳

An upright container, such as a tall can

✳

An artificial flower

✳

Pretty wallpaper or shelf paper

METHOD

Spread a sheet out on a flat surface. Empty out the contents of a messy drawer or cupboard onto the sheet, while singing:

✻

"If I'm rich, or if I'm poor,
I'll find treasure in this drawer.
I will seek a hidden hoard
within the maw of this cupboard.
In my house are treasured friends,
lost among life's odds and ends.
In my search, both short and sweet,
I'll find some gifts and leave it neat."

✻

Thread onto some string anything you find with a ring or handle, then lay the threaded items in a circle on the sheet. Stand anything long in a tall container at the center of the circle. Everyone should add a verse about each item, such as: "Here's a little silver spoon, I'll make it shine just like the Moon." Eventually, you will discover a long-lost trinket—the hidden treasure. Line the drawer or cupboard with paper, return the threaded items, and fasten an artificial flower to the handle to show the magic you have worked.

A traditional spell to restore harmony to the home and make your kitchen a peaceful gathering place for family and friends.

HARMONY in the KITCHEN

Super-potent spell

IN ANCIENT TIMES, THE TASK OF COOKING WAS DONE OVER A FIRE AT THE CENTER OF THE MAIN ROOM IN THE FAMILY'S LIVING SPACE. GRADUALLY, THIS IMPORTANT DOMESTIC TASK BECAME RELEGATED TO A SPECIAL ROOM SET ASIDE FOR FOOD PREPARATION, AWAY FROM THE REST OF THE HOME. TODAY, THE TWO TRADITIONS ARE BEGINNING TO MERGE, AND THE KITCHEN IS BECOMING THE HEART OF THE HOME ONCE AGAIN. HERE IS A SPELL TO ATTRACT PEACE, LOVE, AND FUN INTO THE REALM OF THE KITCHEN.

You will need

Wooden spoons

*

Decorative adornments, such as colored ribbons, artificial flowers, glitter, pictures, and photographs

METHOD

By making your kitchen special to each person who uses it, this room can become a center for harmony and life. Let the family decorate wooden spoons with anything they like, from colored ribbons and glitter to photographs, pictures, colored markers, or anything else you fancy. While you are all decorating the spoons, say, in unison:

"Wooden spoons, hark to me,
stir up peace and harmony.
Bring in joy and love and fun,
through the door, for everyone."

Affix the decorated spoons over your kitchen door to attract love, peace, and joy into this symbolic center of the household. Leave the kitchen and, one at a time, come back in through the door above which the spoons are affixed.

A charm to inspire and promote culinary success.

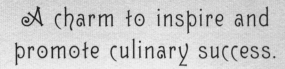

LUCKY SPICES

You will need

A lime or other small citrus fruit, whole cloves, and orrisroot powder

✳

A large-mouthed glass jar with a lid

A small spoon, spices, recipe pictures, and small kitchen implements

✳

Dry white rice

✳

Flour

✳

A white candle

ALTHOUGH SOME COOKS HAVE TO FOLLOW EACH STEP IN A RECIPE BOOK VERY CAREFULLY TO BE SUCCESSFUL, THERE ARE SOME WHO JUST KNOW INTUITIVELY HOW MUCH SALT, SUGAR, OR BAKING TIME A DISH NEEDS TO BE PERFECT, RELYING ON LUCK AND EXPERIENCE FOR RESULTS. HERE IS A COOKING CHARM FOR ACHIEVING THIS KIND OF "EFFORTLESS" CULINARY SUCCESS.

METHOD

Make a pomander by completely studding a lime or some other small citrus fruit with cloves, and dipping it into orrisroot powder. Hang it up to dry completely. Place symbols of the kind of cookery you do into a glass jar—a small spoon, spices, pictures of your favorite dishes, and small kitchen implements, for example. Use dry white rice to fill in the spaces. Place the dried pomander on top of this collection, to ward off disappointments.

Put the lid on the jar and place the jar on your kitchen counter. Form a circle of flour around it, light a white candle, and say:

"Jar of luck, to me
please bring the
flavor to my cooking.
When I give the jar a shake,
bless the stew or bread or cake,
and when my friends come round to eat
may they find my dishes sweet,
whether I boil or roast or bake."

A spell to drive even the most persistent mouse from your home.

PESTS AWAY

SOME WITCHES CLAIM TO BE ABLE TO TALK TO ANIMALS. SOMETIMES THEY ASK THEM FOR HELP, AND SOMETIMES THEY TRY TO PERSUADE THOSE THAT ARE A NUISANCE INTO GOING AWAY. TYPICALLY, THE LANGUAGE OF THE ANIMAL AND THE HERBS AND SPICES THAT THE CREATURES DISLIKE ARE USED. MAGIC IS OFTEN SPOKEN AS WELL, TO MAKE THE SPELL EXTRA EFFECTIVE. HERE IS A SPELL TO HELP YOU GET RID OF EVEN THE MOST DETERMINED MOUSE.

You will need

A picture of a mouse

*

Old-fashioned camphor or mothballs

*

Three black candles

*

Lentils, or any other hard grain that does not appeal to mice

*

A straw broom

METHOD

Get a picture of a mouse and place the camphor or mothballs in a circle around the picture. Light three black candles, set in a triangle around the circle of balls, and pour a ring of lentils, or any other hard grain that does not appeal to mice, around the triangle. Sing, in any tune you wish:

"Mouse, mouse, leave my house,
go from here quite quickly.
Tell your friends they'll meet
swift ends, or end up very sickly.
From each room by power of broom
I sweep you out so neatly.
I send you out, don't turn about,
depart from here completely.
Go now, go now, go now!"

Throw the lentils outside your house, as far away as you can. Place a mothball at each point where the mouse has been spotted. Use a straw broom to sweep a magical circle around the edge of each room where the mouse has been seen, and rest assured that the offending creature will not return.

CHAPTER 5

DREAM WEAVING

❧ ✳ ❧

EVERYONE DREAMS, AND IN MANY WAYS DREAMS
ARE THE DOORWAY TO THE MAGICAL LAYERS OF
YOUR INNER MIND. BY LEARNING TO RECALL DREAMS,
TO UNDERSTAND AND DIRECT THEM, TODAY'S SPELL
WEAVERS CAN ACCESS HUGE AREAS OF POWERFUL
INFORMATION. YOU MAY HAVE FASCINATING
ADVENTURES THAT SHOW YOUR COURAGE, UNVEIL
FORGOTTEN FRIENDSHIPS, BRING SOLUTIONS
TO PROBLEMS, OR SEE INTO THE FUTURE. WITH
PRACTICE YOU CAN CONTROL AND DIRECT THESE
MAGICAL TIMES AND DRAW STRENGTH, INSPIRATION,
AND A SENSE OF WONDER FROM THEM.

MANY OF THE IMAGES, TRANSFORMATIONS, AND
APPLICATIONS OF MAGIC HAPPEN IN ANOTHER DIMENSION,
SOMETIMES CALLED THE "ASTRAL REALM," SO IT IS
IMPORTANT THAT THE SPELLCASTER FINDS WAYS
TO ACCESS THIS PLACE OF VISION.

FINDING INSIGHT in DREAMS

THE DOOR OF DREAMS

Everyone has the mental tools to reach into this dimension within their subconscious or inner minds, but bringing back clear memories and impressions requires practice. The subconscious guards its secrets, and magic workers have to find the key that will unlock this hidden treasure chest of vision. The way in is through the door of dreams, not just the spontaneous ones at night, but daydreams, meditations, and inner journeys all can help make a clear and usable connection to these inner worlds.

THE DREAM DIARY

Although some people don't remember their dreams, everyone does dream during sleep. One of the best ways of unlocking the door of dreams and memories is by the use of a dream diary. Any book will do, so long as it is always to be found, with a working pen, near the sleeper's bed. Immediately on waking, even in the middle of the night, it is essential to get into the habit of writing down memories, impressions, or just fleeting images from the dream, no matter how vague. During the day other fragments may come to you and should also be jotted down. Gradually memories get clearer and more detailed. Our dreams may predict the future, or offer solutions to problems, but unless they are recalled in the morning no use can be made of this knowledge.

Record your dreams in a diary whenever you can recall them.

DECIPHERING DREAMS

As well as showing aspects of another dimension, our dreams reveal their contents by use of images, symbols, and sometimes jokes. Although there are lots of books that aim to explain the meanings of dream symbols, these are often personal.

A Native American dream catcher may help you to recall your dreams.

Dreaming of gifts: a surprise on its way or feeling boxed in?

For example, a dream of a gift may be seen in terms of a spiritual gift, such as healing, or interpreted as a present, indicating that the dreamer should concentrate on the present time. Others might see the gift as a box containing a pleasant surprise, or as a symbol of a protected place, or even being boxed in.

Whatever the reading, dreams have to be recalled before they can be understood, and the following spells will help you come to grips with these hidden aspects of your sleeping mind. Although catching hold of your dreams may seem very hard at first, it is well worth continuing to recall at least part of a dream each time you wake. Some people find using a Native American dream catcher can help. It may also help if you have a friend who you can talk to about your dreams, perhaps exchanging ideas and insights. Sometimes groups of friends find they are sharing symbols, characters, or other aspects of action in their dreams. As you discover more you will also be discovering parts of the hidden side of you, where you may well have characteristics that you feel you lack in real life. If, in dreams, you can solve problems or overcome monsters, what is stopping you from doing the same when you are awake? Try, and you might be surprised at your own power.

DREAMING WHILE AWAKE

Magic also relies on waking dreams, induced through meditation, daydreaming, and creative visualization, for it is by these means we are able to talk to our inner selves, to receive guidance, help, and inspiration. The spells in this chapter are aimed at awakening a clearer connection between waking and sleeping minds, so that dreams can be remembered and their contents used.

Use meditation to induce a dream state while awake.

A spell to ensure that your dream memories stay with you in your waking hours.

✳

You will need

Paper and a pen

✳

A piece of plain cotton, about 20 x 10 inches (50 x 25cm)

✳

White thread and needle

✳

Dried jasmine flowers, hops, poppy petals, rose petals, and lavender flowers

✳

One black candle, one white candle, and two silver candles

MOON SLEEP SPELL

SLEEP ANALYSTS BELIEVE THAT DREAMS ENCAPSULATE DIFFERENT ASPECTS OF OUR PSYCHE AND CIRCUMSTANCES, INCLUDING OUR LIFE SITUATIONS, RELATIONSHIPS, AND EXPERIENCES. IF THIS IS TRUE, THEN AN AWARENESS OF OUR DREAMS CAN HELP US TO UNDERSTAND OUR THOUGHTS AND EMOTIONS. UNFORTUNATELY, WE CANNOT ALWAYS REMEMBER OUR DREAMS, BUT WITH THE HELP OF THIS SPELL, YOU CAN ENHANCE YOUR LEVEL OF DREAM PERCEPTION.

METHOD

Record your dreams from recent nights as best you can.
Find out what phase the Moon was in each night—this tells
you during which phases you best recall your dreams—and record
this information as well. Sew a small pillow from cotton, about
10 x 5 inches (25 x 13cm), and loosely fill it with dried flowers
associated with the Moon (see opposite). On the evening of a
new moon, light one black, one white, and two silver candles
to represent the Moon's phases: dark, new, waxing, and waning.
Place the dream pillow under your normal pillow and say this spell:

✳

> "Flowers of magic, flowers of sleep,
> let my moon-dream visions
> creep into my memory to keep.
> Show to me in bright day's light
> all the adventures of the night."

✳

Note every dream you can recall—even
fragments—for at least two months. You will
find that your memory will begin to
improve, and that patterns
in your dreams will
start to emerge.

A spell to drive nightmares away and return peace and restfulness to your slumber.

NIGHTMARES AWAY

NIGHTMARES OR VIOLENT DREAMS HAPPEN TO MOST PEOPLE AT SOME TIME IN THEIR LIVES, AND CAN BE VERY UNPLEASANT. MANY PEOPLE EXPERIENCE THESE UNPLEASANT DREAMS WHEN THEY ARE UNDER STRESS, OR GOING THROUGH A CHANGE IN THEIR LIFE PATTERN. THIS SPELL

CAN BE USED TO DISCOURAGE NIGHTMARES, AND TO ENCOURAGE A GOOD NIGHT'S SLEEP. IT IS BEST PERFORMED DURING A WANING MOON.

You will need

A violet or purple candle

A copper coin and a silver coin

＊

A small stone or pebble

＊

A white cord at least 16 yards (14.5m) long

METHOD

Light a violet candle—the color violet helps attract the power of the Moon. Put a copper coin on the floor under the top left-hand corner of your bed, a silver coin under the top right-hand corner, and a small stone or pebble under the bed, in the center. Fasten one end of a length of white cord to the top right-hand corner of the bed. Carefully wind the cord around your bed, clockwise, so that it lies on the floor surrounding it. As you do this, sing or say:

* ✳ *

"This cord I wind, all fears to bind,
and from my dreams
drive out all nightmare scenes,
all shouts and screams
'til daylight shines about."

* ✳ *

Tie the end of the cord to wherever it finishes up, to complete the circle. As you go to bed each night, mentally visualize the objects around the bed and know they will bring calm and safety, repeating the rhyme if necessary.

A spell to summon those you are missing into your dreams.

SWEET DREAMS

IF YOU RECOGNIZE THAT THE PEOPLE YOU LOVE WHO ARE FAR AWAY FROM YOU CAN SEE THE SAME SKY, THE SAME MOON, AND UNLESS THEY ARE IN THE OTHER HEMISPHERE OF THE WORLD, THE SAME STAR PATTERNS AS YOU, THIS CAN HELP YOU FEEL CLOSER TO THEM. SENDING A SPELL FOR A STAR TO SHINE ON THOSE YOU MISS AND TO INSPIRE A DREAM OF THEM WILL ALSO HELP BRING THEM PSYCHICALLY CLOSER TO YOU.

You will need

A picture of those whom you miss

*

A silver picture frame

*

Small self-adhesive stars

METHOD

When it is dark outside, search the night sky for a star. If you cannot actually see any, imagine one. Picture the faces, voices, and presence of those you miss, laughing in the sky around the star. Imagine them seeing the star and noticing your face and voice too. Chant this spell to bring sweet dreams of those you miss:

"Starlight, star bright,
bring sweet dreams to me tonight.
Sweet heart, though we're apart,
know you're always in my heart.
Starlight and moonbeams,
bring my lover in my dreams,
so we can shine together, please.
This will bring my sore soul ease."

Keep a picture of the person or persons you miss in a silver frame and place it on the windowsill, so that starlight can fall on it and bring you sweet dreams of them. Stick a few self-adhesive stars on or around the picture every night, until you are together again.

Super-potent spell

A spell to help you dream about whatever you wish.

SYMBOLIC DREAM POWER

ONCE YOU HAVE BECOME ADEPT AT
REMEMBERING YOUR DREAMS AND MAKING
NOTES ON ANY SYMBOLS APPEARING IN THEM
(SEE THE MOON SLEEP SPELL, PAGES 126–127),
YOU CAN USE THE POWER OF DREAMS TO HELP
BRING ABOUT MAGICAL OUTCOMES
IN YOUR LIFE.

You will need

**A book to use as
a dream diary**

**A book on
dream symbols**

✳

**Images of the
symbols of magic
you want your
mind to listen to**

METHOD

Decipher dream symbols with a book on dreams. Picture symbols that you wish to enter your dreams. Common ones include:

A house represents your life; hidden rooms are unexplored areas. Visualize a house with an open door to exploit hidden talents.

A bird symbolizes travel or flight. Look at a picture of a bird and some real feathers before you sleep to dream of journeys.

A crowd applauding suggests success. Visualize such a crowd and your dreams may lead to success.

Sing this spell before you sleep to encourage your desired dream images:

⇜ ✳ ⇝

"As 1 fall into the arms of sleep,
and shadows in the twilight creep,
let mind be calm and pictures rise,
and deep-set insights make me wise.
If 1 ask a dream to show the path
1 tread, the way to go, or if some
other aid 1 need, from sleeping soul
send out with speed."

A daydreaming spell to help you solve your problems and release stress.

❋

DREAMING the DAY AWAY

IN THIS MODERN, HECTIC WORLD, OUR
HURRIED LIFESTYLE ENCOURAGES THE
BUILD-UP OF DESTRUCTIVE CHEMICALS
IN OUR SYSTEM, WHICH IN TURN CAN
LEAD TO ILLNESS OR DISCOMFORT.
THIS SPELL HELPS YOU TO SET ASIDE
A FEW MINUTES EVERY DAY FOR
DAYDREAMING, TO HELP YOU
OVERCOME STRESS AND TO GUIDE
YOU TOWARD THE SOLUTIONS
TO YOUR PROBLEMS.

METHOD

Cut out a circle of silver paper (silver will attract the powers of the Moon) and lay it on a soft surface. Use a ballpoint pen to write your initials on the back of the paper in mirror writing, so that when you turn the circle over the letters stand out. Light an incense stick and place your hands on each side of the circle. Focus on the most wonderful location you know—somewhere you have already visited, or somewhere you wish to go. Let the image flood through you.

You will need

Silver paper or foil

✳

Scissors

✳

Ballpoint pen

✳

Incense stick with a relaxing scent

Become aware of a doorway or natural cave in the scene. Go toward it. Inside it will be light, together with a change of scene. This new scene will involve a problem you are trying to solve. As you look around, you will see clues to how the problem can be solved.

Allow your mind to drift over these clues, taking in possible solutions. After a few moments, bring your attention back to the present and note how relaxed and calm you are. Recall the details of the problem and its solution.

A magical charm
to bring forth inner
guidance while you sleep.

≈ ✳ ≈

WEB of DREAMS

NATIVE AMERICAN IN ORIGIN, DREAM
CATCHERS ARE TYPICALLY MADE FROM
A CIRCLE OF THIN TWIG WRAPPED IN
COLORED THREADS WITH A NET WOVEN
IN THE CENTER. THEIR PURPOSE IS TO
CATCH POSITIVE DREAMS, WHILE LETTING
NEGATIVE DREAMS PASS THROUGH.
DREAM WEBS ARE MADE IN A SLIGHTLY
DIFFERENT WAY, AND THEIR PURPOSE IS
DIFFERENT AS WELL: THEY CAN INDUCE
A STATE OF DREAMING WHEREIN INNER
GUIDANCE IS DISCOVERED. HERE IS HOW
TO MAKE A DREAM WEB.

METHOD

Cut out a circle of stiff cardboard. Either leave it as a disk or cut out an inner circle so that you have a cardboard ring. With silver thread, sew across the circle, making spokes, as on a wheel. Secure a few colored threads in the center of the "wheel" and wind each thread around each spoke in a clockwise spiral. Decorate the cardboard with glitter powder or paint, and attach bright beads or other ornaments. As you make the web, say:

You will need

Stiff cardboard (not corrugated), 8 inches (20cm) wide

✳

Scissors or a craft knife

✳

Silver, blue, white, light green, and pink thread, and a needle

✳

Glitter powder or paint

✳

Small, light ornaments, such as beads, feathers, or tassels

✳

Cord

"My dreams will be sweet
and as I sleep, the powers
of blessing will find me.
My rest shall be calm,
in slumber's arms,
and troubles shall all
fall behind me."

Braid a cord using the colored threads and hang the web above the pillow of your bed. As you settle down to sleep, mentally trace the spirals of the web one at a time until you feel relaxed. Feel yourself float off into the starry realm of your dreams to receive the guidance that awaits you.

A spell for communicating with those you have lost.

~ ✳ ~

A Letter from Your Soul

OFTEN WHEN SOMEONE CLOSE TO US HAS DIED OR MOVED AWAY, WE FEEL LIKE WE NEVER ADEQUATELY EXPRESSED OUR LOVE, THANKS, REGRETS, OR EVEN APOLOGIES TO THAT PERSON. MANY MAGIC WORKERS BELIEVE IN THE LAW OF KARMA, WHICH ENTAILS ACCEPTING RESPONSIBILITY FOR ALL YOUR ACTIONS, GOOD AND BAD. IF YOU HAVE HURT PEOPLE OR NEVER PROPERLY SHOWED YOUR LOVE AND AFFECTION, THIS CAN LEAVE KARMIC DEBTS. BY WRITING A SOUL LETTER, YOU MAY BE ABLE TO REPAY THOSE DEBTS.

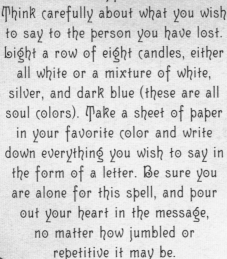

METHOD

Think carefully about what you wish to say to the person you have lost. Light a row of eight candles, either all white or a mixture of white, silver, and dark blue (these are all soul colors). Take a sheet of paper in your favorite color and write down everything you wish to say in the form of a letter. Be sure you are alone for this spell, and pour out your heart in the message, no matter how jumbled or repetitive it may be.

You will need

Eight candles, either all white or a mixture of white, silver, and dark blue

✳

Your favorite colored writing paper and a pen

✳

Paints, glitter, or other decorative materials

✳

A fireproof container, such as a metal bucket or deep tray

You will probably feel very emotional, and writing your letter might make you cry. Take your time writing, decorating and finally signing the paper. When you are sure it is complete, carefully set fire to it in a fireproof container and watch it burn to ashes. Crush and sprinkle the ashes in the earth or into a river, or let the wind carry them away from a high window. Know that your message will reach its recipient soon.

A calming brew to help lull you to sleep and to bring clear dreams.

*

DREAM TEA

THROUGHOUT HISTORY ALMOST EVERY CULTURE HAS USED HERBS FOR VARIOUS PURPOSES; EVERY REGION HAD ITS HELPFUL PLANTS FOR EASING PAIN, COOLING FEVERS, ALLEVIATING SICKNESS, AND ENCOURAGING SLEEP. TODAY, MANY OF THESE PLANTS ARE COMMONLY FOUND IN HERBAL AND HEALTH FOOD STORES, SO IT IS SAFE FOR NOVICES TO USE THEM. ALWAYS BE SURE YOU HAVE THE RIGHT HERB FOR YOUR PARTICULAR CONDITION, THOUGH, AND ALWAYS BUY FROM A REPUTABLE SOURCE. HERE IS A SAFE, SIMPLE, AND EFFECTIVE BREW TO HELP YOU SLEEP AND TO BRING CLEAR DREAMS.

You will need

1 tsp. dried camomile flowers and ½ tsp. dried peppermint leaves

*

Powdered ginger and nutmeg

*

A bowl, spoon, strainer, and mug

*

Runny honey and fresh lemon juice

METHOD

To make a cup of dream tea, put 1 tsp. of dried camomile flowers, $\frac{1}{2}$ tsp. of dried peppermint leaves, a pinch of powdered ginger, and a pinch of powdered nutmeg into a bowl. Add $\frac{1}{2}$ pint (300ml) of boiling water. Allow to infuse for about five minutes, stirring it a few times and singing:

"Sweet herbs, sleep herbs, mixed in this tea, fill me and thrill me with bright dreams to see. Make it taste nice with flowers and spice, and the addition of lemon and honey."

Strain the mixture into a clean mug. You can drink this brew warm or cool, with lemon and honey added to taste. A small amount will help sleep come to you sooner, and will help you dream more clearly.

INDEX

A

Age of Aquarius 94
air (element) 25, 26–29,
36–37
amulets 9
ancestors, spell for
connecting with 64–65
Aquarius 94–95
Aries 74–75
astrology 42–45, 70–73

B

beauty, spell for
appreciating 76–77

C

Cancer 80–81
Capricorn 92–93
career, spells for success in
56–57, 92–93
charms 9, 10, 12, 99
collective unconscious 64
colors 12, 27, 74–75,
82–83, 104–105
planetary 10–11, 43,
46–47, 48–49, 50–51,
52–53, 56–57, 58–59,
66–67
soul 139
concentration 15, 22–23
confidence, spell for 82–83
cooking, spell for success
in 116–117
courage, spells for 54–55,
74–75

D

daydreaming 125,
134–135
days of the week 43–45,
46–47, 48–49, 50–51,
52–53, 54–55, 56–57,
58–59, 66–67
decision-making, spell for
86–87
desires, spell for achieving
96–97
dreams 8, 121, 122–125,
130–131, 136–137
remembering 122, 123,
126–127
symbols 132–133

E

earth (element) 25, 26–29,
30–31
electronic equipment,
spell for protecting
60–61
elements 25, 26–29
see also individual
elements
emotions 32–33, 88–89,
138–139
energies/forces/powers
8, 14–17, 44–45, 69,
102–103

F

fire (element) 25, 26–29,
34–35
flowers and plants 43–44,
48–49, 52–53, 54–55,
72–73, 92–93, 126–127

G

Gemini 78–79
gods and goddesses
10–11, 14, 41, 82–83,
84–85
see also individual deities
guidance 125, 136–137

H

harmony in the kitchen,
spell for 114–115
harvest spell 84–85
healing 8, 101–103
helping spell 94–95
herbs and spices 99,
100–101, 104–105,
106–107, 108–109,
110–111, 116–117,
140–141
horoscope 70–71

I

influences, planetary
42–45, 70–73
chart 67
inner powers 14–15,
18–19, 46–47, 48–49,
62–63
insight, spells for 20–21,
48–49

J

Jupiter 10–11, 42–44,
56–57

L

Leo 82–83
Libra 86–87
love and friendship, spells
for 52–53, 78–79,
130–131, 138–139
luck 9, 12, 66–67, 99, 103

M

magical world, connecting
with 22–23
Mars 10–11, 42–45, 54–55
meditation 15–17, 122

memory, spell for
   improving 106–107
Mercury 10–11, 42–45,
   50–51, 78
metals 10
   planetary 43, 54–55, 57,
   67, 89
money 12, 104–105
Moon 10–11, 42–45,
   48–49, 89, 126–127,
   128–129, 135

N
natural materials 9, 26,
   27, 43, 44, 84–85
nature, powers of 102–103
Neptune 42–43, 62–63
nightmares, preventing
   128–129
numbers 12
   planetary 43, 66–67

P
pentagram 9
pests, spell for getting
   rid of 118–119
Pisces 96–97
planets 10–11, 41, 42–45,
   66–67, 70–71
   see also individual planets
plants see flowers and
   plants
Pluto 42–43, 64–65
preparation 28, 103
problem-solving 16,
   36–37, 86–87, 121,
   123, 134–135
protection, spell for 80–81
psychic abilities, spells to
   activate 48–49, 62–63

♐
relaxation 17, 22–23,
   134–135

♒
sacred space 28–29,
   38–39, 85, 108–109
safe journey, spell for
   50–51
Sagittarius 90–91
Saturn 10–11, 42–44,
   58–59
scents 10, 12, 22–23, 28,
   36–37
   planetary 43, 50–51,
   56–57
Scorpio 88–89
self-awareness, spells for
   18–19, 20–21
sleep, spell for 140–141
spell, definition of 9
spices see herbs and spices
spirit (element) 25, 26–29,
   38–39
sport, spell for success in
   90–91
subconscious 16–17,
   122–125
Sun 10–11, 42–45, 46–47
super-potent spells 66–67,
   114–115, 132–133
symbols 9, 10–11, 12,
   72–73, 84–85
   astrological 78–79, 82–83
   dream 123–125,
   132–133
   planetary 43, 44, 52–53,
   66–67

♈
talismans 9, 57, 66–67
Taurus 76–77
teas 100–101, 140–141
time 69, 70–73
   spells for mastering
   58–59, 110–111
treasure, spell to find
   112–113

☋
Uranus 42–43, 60–61

♉
Venus 10–11, 42–43,
   52–53
Virgo 84–85
visualization 16–17, 125

♏
water (element) 25, 26–29,
   32–33
wisdom, spell for
   increasing 108–109

♌
zodiac 11, 69, 70–73

CREDITS

We would like to thank and acknowledge the following for supplying images reproduced in this book:

Key: l (left), r (right), a (above), b (below), c (center)

www.shutterstock.com: pp.1–3 (background, also on pp.24–25, 40–41, 68–69, 98–99 & 120–121) andreasnikolas, hsunny & MaxShutter; p.1 (wand) My Portfolio; p.2 (woman) whiteisthecolor; p.3 (book) lady-luck; p.4al fersusart; p.5bl Vera Petruk; p.7a Irina Vaneeva; p.8ar MicroOne; p.8bl Vera Petruk; p.9a Fribus Mara; p.9b MicroOne; pp.10–11 (table background, also on pp.57, 67 & 71) javarman; p.11ac MorePics; p.11ar Natalia Lyubova; p.12 Vector Tradition; p.13b Tatiana Apanasova; p.15b Annykos; p.16a MSSA; p.19l Kamieshkova; p.21 (map) Tetiana Ch; p.21 (pens) ArtMari; p.22 Kamieshkova; p.23a zhekakopylov; p.25 (pentagram) SvedOliver; p.26 Vera Petruk; p.27a Egor Shilov; p.27c N_Melanchenko; p.27b Kamieshkova; p.28a N_Melanchenko; p.29 (stone) Egor Shilov; p.29 (incense & candles) N_Melanchenko; p.29 (compass) Navalnyi; p.31 (stones) Egor Shilov; p.35b chempina; p.37bl N_Melanchenko; p.39 (stone) Egor Shilov; p.39 (incense & candle) zhekakopylov; p.40 (wolf) Croisy; p.41 (Moon) Dotted Yeti; p.42b Katja Gerasimova; p.60a MSSA; p.61 (wand) fersusart; p.63b Asya Illustra; p.65 anemad; p.67a Uncle Leo; p.68 (owl) rudall30; p.69 (sundial) 3Dsculptor; p.75br chempina; p.79 Vector Tradition; p.93 owatta; p.99 (cauldron) Pagina; p.103 Cozy nook; p.106b Vector Tradition; p.119b chempina; p.121 (feather) mycteria; p.123a annamiro; p.123b pimchawee; p.124a AmamiArt; p.125 aninata; p.128b Kamieshkova; p.130bl helgascandinavus; p.136a Richard Laschon; p.136b Irina Vaneeva; p.139al Kamieshkova; p.141 (honey & bee) Slonomysh.

All other photographs and illustrations are the copyright of Quarto Publishing plc. While every effort has been made to credit contributors, Quarto would like to apologize should there have been any omissions or errors—and would be pleased to make the appropriate correction for future editions of the book.